D0890750

ON

KIERKEGAARD

Susan Leigh Anderson
University of Connecticut

Wadsworth
Thomson Learning™

Australia • Canada • Denmark • Japan • Mexico • New Zealand • Philippines
Puerto Rico • Singapore • Spain • United Kingdom • United States

To Michael, who has taught me how to "live well,"
and to Alex, who is still trying to find his way.

I would also like to thank Sondra Melzer for her
help and moral support.

Printed in the United States of America
1 2 3 4 5 6 7 03 02 01 00 99

For permission to use material from this text, contact us:
Web: www.thomsonrights.com
Fax: 1-800-730-2215
Phone: 1-800-730-2214

For more information, contact:
Wadsworth/Thomson Learning
10 Davis Drive
Belmont, CA 94002-3098
USA
www.wadsworth.com

ISBN: 0-534-57601-X

Contents

I

Kierkegaard's Life

My whole life is an epigram calculated to make people aware.
(*Journal*, 1848)

Søren Kierkegaard was born in Copenhagen, Denmark on May 5, 1813, the seventh and youngest child of Michael Pedersen Kierkegaard and his second wife Ane Sørensdatter Lund Kierkegaard. Outwardly, Kierkegaard's life was rather uneventful. Except for four visits to Berlin, a brief trip across the sound to Sweden and a pilgrimage to his father's birthplace in rural Denmark, he spent the short forty-two years of his life in Copenhagen. He sowed his wild oats as a university student before becoming religious. He fell in love with, and became engaged to, Regina Olsen and then, inexplicably, broke off the relationship. Although he studied to become a Lutheran pastor, he chose to spend an essentially withdrawn life as an author, appearing in public only to take walks and carriage rides. He also involved himself in two public controversies: he denounced the low standards of the popular Copenhagen satirical paper *The Corsair*, which in turn caricatured Kierkegaard unmercifully, and he attacked the Danish Lutheran Church. He died on November 11, 1855, refusing to receive the sacrament from a pastor.

Inwardly, however, much more was going on in Kierkegaard's life, which affected and was affected by his philosophy. One tenet of his philosophy was that you can't tell much about a person from outward behavior; what is really important is not publicly observable. Inside Kierkegaard:

> ...his life was one of the most dramatic ever known, because of the depth and power of his "reflection." Everything took place inside his soul, and what others would regard as trivial, or to be forgotten as soon as possible, was in him enhanced and magnified and "penetrated" by thought until it yielded the richest of poetic and philosophical treasures....Here is...an individual man, highly gifted but terribly "alone," struggling not with external forces, but with himself — and God.[1]

The place to begin to understand Kierkegaard's life is with his father, who greatly influenced him. Michael Pedersen Kierkegaard (1756-1838) was born into a poor family in Jutland, one of the bleakest parts of Denmark. He spent his youth there as a shepherd boy. When he was eleven, he was sent to Copenhagen to live as an apprentice with fairly well-to-do relatives who saw to it that he received religious guidance of a rural type (they too had recently left Jutland), with an anti-clerical undercurrent, which profoundly affected him for the rest of his life and which he in turn passed on to his children.

Coming to Copenhagen greatly altered the course of Michael Pedersen Kierkegaard's life. He was an excellent and ambitious apprentice, and the economic conditions in Copenhagen at the time were extremely favorable. The young man quickly acquired his own dry goods business and invested the profits wisely. By his thirties, the former shepherd boy was a very wealthy man; but there was a tension in him between his rural roots and new urban surroundings. He was, also, reputed to be a profoundly melancholy man.

There are two theories about the source of this melancholia. Some biographers believe it had its origins in his having once cursed God as a child. According to this theory, he was troubled by his youthful impiety for the rest of his life and believed his success in life was evidence of God's mocking him. Other biographers claim the source of his melancholy lay in his feeling guilty about having impregnated his housekeeper, Ana Sørensdatter Lund, less than a year after the death of

---

[1] Robert Bretall, *A Kierkegaard Anthology*, Princeton University Press, Princeton, N.J., 1973, p. 1.

his first wife. He quickly married the peasant housekeeper who became the mother of all seven of his children.

In any case, about the time of this second marriage, he put his business into the hands of trustees and retired to brood over his sins. His interest in business and his financial acumen didn't entirely leave him however. Sixteen years later, he transferred most of his capital into guaranteed gold-convertible bonds and managed not only to hang on to his fortune, but even to increase it relative to others, during the disastrous state bankruptcy of 1813, the year in which Søren Kierkegaard was born.

Søren, a somewhat frail and sheltered child, spent much time in the company of his strict and eccentric father who subjected his family to large doses of religion, inculcating an emotional, anxiety-ridden religious devotion into his son. He also awakened young Søren's imagination by constantly acting out stories and scenes. His *nouveau riche* father sent him to Copenhagen's finest preparatory school in 1821; yet, revealing his peasant upbringing, he forced petty economies on his son. Søren's unstylish wardrobe caused him to stand out painfully among his aristocratic fellow pupils. He was a bright, although not particularly conscientious student known for his sharp wit. One of his classmates later summed up Kierkegaard's relationship with his fellow students and teachers:

> S.K. was viewed by his fellow students as a witty fellow with whom it was dangerous to quarrel, because he knew how to make his opponent appear ridiculous. They also viewed him as a fundamentally good boy, religious and moral, and they did not tease him about this....We did not have the least suspicion that he would one day come forth as a great opponent of his times. He seemed to be very conservative.... The teachers acknowledged that S.K. was unusually gifted, but were not always satisfied with him. They believed him lacking in diligence, and he sometimes treated them with impudence. One time the late L.C. Müller, our Hebrew teacher, corrected him rather sharply, and when S.K. broke out into loud laughter, Müller, who knew him from the family home, buttoned up his coat and said with great anger, "Either you will leave or I will." After a moment's consideration S.K. replied, "Well then, it's best that I leave." And he left.[1]

---

[1] Peter Engel Lind, letter to H.P. Barfod, September 16, 1869, in

Søren Kierkegaard
(From a drawing by Christian Kierkegaard)

In 1930, at the age of seventeen, Kierkegaard went to the University of Copenhagen, enrolling in a theological course of study as his father wished and as his brother Peter Christian had done before him; but he spent most of his time reading literature and philosophy. At the University, he was confronted with the Hegelian system and reacted strongly against it. Having no place for the individual, it could not supply what he was looking for —"a truth which is true *for me...the idea for which I can live and die*."[1] Neither could contemporary Danish Lutheranism provide what he was looking for. Søren ceased to practice his religion and he embarked on a life of pleasure, revolting against both his father and God. A melancholy which originated in his childhood haunted him, however. He recorded in his *Journal*:

> I have just returned from a party of which I was the life and soul; wit poured from my lips, everyone laughed and admired me — but I went away — and the dash should be as long as the world's orbit ——————————————— and wanted to shoot myself.

Encounters with Kierkegaard, A Life as Seen by His Contemporaries, edited by Bruce H. Kirmmse, Princeton University Press, Princeton, N.J., 1996 p. 11.
[1] Kierkegaard's *Journal*, 1835, quoted in Bretall, *Op. Cit.*, p. 5.

'Sdeath, I can abstract from everything but not from
myself. I cannot even forget myself when I am asleep.[1]

Even as he was floundering, Kierkegaard knew that the key to a
contented life lay not in others' approval, but in getting to know
himself, and that struggling to find oneself could be a good thing:

> One must know oneself before knowing anything else. It is
> only after a man has thus understood himself inwardly and has
> thus seen his way, that life acquires peace and significance....
> in the spiritual world it is first of all necessary to work for
> some time before the light bursts through and the sun shines
> forth in all its glory.[2]

A gradual return to Christianity culminated, in 1838, in a
thorough reconciliation with his father on his birthday (May 5th), and
two weeks later (May 19th) "the sun [shone] forth in all its glory" for
Kierkegaard when he had a religious conversion experience of
"indescribable joy."

His father died soon after (August 9th), leaving Søren a
considerable fortune. With the death of both his father and his teacher
and moral mentor, philosophy professor Poul Martin Møller, in 1838,
Søren decided to apply himself seriously to the study of theology and
to become a pastor. In that same year his first work of substance
appeared, *From the Papers of One Still Living*, a scathing attack on his
contemporary Hans Christian Andersen, in which Kierkegaard
maintained that Andersen's work was marred by a self-pitying
sentimentality and was completely lacking the idea of an autonomous,
responsible human being.

Kierkegaard passed his theological examinations in July of 1840
cum laude and, in the next year, finished his doctoral dissertation, *On
the Concept of Irony*, in which modern romantic irony is negatively
contrasted with the irony of Socrates, one of Kierkegaard's heroes.

Shortly after passing his theological examinations (September,
1840), Kierkegaard became engaged to Regine Olsen, the pretty
seventeen-year-old daughter of State Councilor Terkild Olsen, who —
after God — was the love of his life. He had met her years before at the
home of a friend and, according to his own later account of his

---

[1] *Journal*, 1836, quoted in Bretall, *Op. Cit.*, p. 7.
[2] *Journal*, 1835, quoted in Bretall, *Op. Cit.*, p. 6.

Regine Olsen
(From a photograph in the Picture Collection of the Royal Library, Copenhagen)

relationship with Regine[1], even before his father's death he "had decided upon her." During the time that he studied for his examinations, he "let her being penetrate [his]." He found excuses to visit the family and on September 8th, he took advantage of an opportunity to see her alone to let her know how he felt about her:

> We met each other on the street outside their house. She said there was nobody at home. I was foolhardy enough to look upon that as an invitation, just the opportunity I wanted. I went in with her. We stood alone in the living room. She was a little uneasy. I asked her to play something as she usually did. She did so; but that did not help me. Then suddenly I took the music away and closed it, not without a certain violence, threw it down upon the piano and said: "Oh, what do I care about music now! It is you I am searching for, it is you whom I have sought after for two years." She was silent. I did nothing else to make an impression upon her; I even warned her against myself, against my melancholy....
>
> She remained quite silent. At last I left, for I was anxious lest someone should come and find both of us, and she so disturbed. I went immediately to [State Councilor] Olsen. I know that I was terribly concerned that I had made too great

---

[1] *Journal*, 1841, quoted in Bretall, *Op. Cit.*, pp. 14-18.

an impression upon her....

Her father said neither yes nor no, but he was willing enough, as I could see. I asked for a meeting: it was granted to me for the afternoon of the 10th. I did not say a single word to persuade her. She said, Yes.

...But inwardly, the next day I saw that I had made a false step.[1]

Why he felt that he had made a "false step," when he clearly was so in love with Regine, has been the subject of much speculation. He had won "his heart's desire"[2] and gotten Regine to forget about another man, Frederik Schlegel, with whom she'd had a previous attachment ("let that relationship be a parenthesis," Kierkegaard told her); yet as time went by he increasingly believed that he had to end the relationship. In his *Journal*, he said this about his feelings for Regine and why he couldn't marry her:

I cannot decide clearly what purely emotional impression she made upon me. One thing is certain: that she gave herself to me, almost worshipping me, asking me to love her, which moved me to such an extent that I was willing to risk all for her. How much I loved her is shown by the fact that I always tried to hide from myself how much she moved me.... If I had not been a penitent, had not had [my past life], had not been melancholy, my union with her would have made me happier than I had ever dreamed of being. But insofar as I was what, alas, I was, I had to say that I could be happier in my unhappiness without her than with her....

But there was a divine protest, that is how I understood it.[3]

Apparently he felt that he had to give up Regine because he believed, at that time, that he had to choose between Regine and God[4]

---

[1] *Ibid.*, p. 15.

[2] In a letter to Emil Boesen, 1842, quoted in Bretall, *Op. Cit.*, p. 18.

[3] In Bretall, *Op. Cit.*, p. 16.

[4] Not only is this suggested by his own writings, but this is what Regine believed. She gave this statement to Hanne Mourier in 1896: "Kierkegaard's motivation for the break was his conception of his religious task; he dared not bind himself to anyone on earth in order not

— "the thing is not to have many thoughts, but to hold fast to *one* thought"[1] — and he had already chosen God, so he made a "false step" in proposing to her. Later he decided that he had made a mistake in giving up Regine, that if he had had more faith in God, really believing that with God all things are possible, he could have had her too.[2] (More on this, when we turn to a discussion of *Fear and Trembling*.)

It was very difficult ending the relationship. Engagements were not broken easily in those days, especially when one did not have a "good" reason for ending it. In the end, Kierkegaard had to resort to cruelty to force Regine to give up her hold on him. When she asked him, "Are you never going to marry?," he answered, "Yes, perhaps in ten years' time when I have sown my wild oats; then I shall need some young blood to rejuvenate me."[3] What was really going on inside him, he later recorded in his *Journal*:

> It was a time of terrible suffering: to have to be so cruel and at the same time to love as I did. She fought like a tigress. If I had not believed that God had lodged a veto she would have been victorious.[4]

They had one more meeting:

> She said: "Promise to think of me." I did so. "Kiss me," she said. I did so, but without passion. Merciful God!
> And so we parted. I spent the whole night crying on my bed.[5]

---

to be obstructed from his calling. He had to sacrifice the very best thing he owned in order to work as God demanded of him: therefore he sacrificed his love for [me] for the sake of his writing." (quoted in Kirmmse, *Op. Cit.*, pp. 36-7)

[1] *Journal*, 1841, in Bretall, *Op. Cit.*, p. 14. This is what he later called "purity of heart."

[2] In a *Journal* entry, written in 1843, he said: "If I had had faith, I should have remained with Regina." (Quoted by Bretall, *Op. Cit.*, p. 126.)

[3] *Journal*, 1841, quoted in Bretall, *Op. Cit.*, p.17

[4] *Ibid.*

[5] *Ibid.*, p. 18.

Regine became very ill after the engagement was broken off. Two years later she married Frederik Schlegel. Regine and Kierkegaard had only one more brief encounter "for the last time here on earth,"[1] on the street, just before the Schlegels moved to the West Indies where her husband was appointed governor.

Kierkegaard never stopped loving Regine. He wrote most of his books for her and in the end left all he possessed to her, still thinking of himself as engaged to her.[2] For her part, according to a friend, "Regine never forgot the great experience of her early youth. Even though it to some extent had been over her head, the sense of having been face to face with the exceptional, the rare, was never extinguished."[3]

After his broken engagement, Kierkegaard took refuge temporarily in Berlin where he attended Schelling's anti-Hegelian lectures, which were disappointing to him, and worked on a strange enigmatic work — *Either/Or* — that, although published under the pseudonym Victor Eremita, made him famous, in part because of the infamous section "Diary of the Seducer" which introduced a character who "could pretty well qualify as the most ultra-refined 'wolf' in all literature."[4] He returned home to Copenhagen and began to lead an essentially withdrawn life as a writer of independent means — he never became a pastor — living on the diminishing capital left by his father.

The two-volume work *Either/Or* was published in early 1843. The title, according to Walter Lowrie, was perhaps even more important than the book itself. It later became a slogan for Existentialism and Kierkegaard is quite properly regarded as the "Father of Existentialism." "Either/Or" was Kierkegaard's response to Hegel's

---

[1] Regine's account, in Kirmmse, *Op. Cit.*, p. 38.

[2] His will read:

> It is naturally my will that my former fiancée, Mrs. Regine Schlegel, should inherit unconditionally what little I leave behind. If she herself refuses to accept it, it is to be offered to her on the condition that she acts as trustee for its distribution to the poor.
>
> What I wish to express is that for me an engagement was and is just as binding as a marriage, and that therefore my estate is to revert to her in exactly the same manner as if I had been married to her. (Kirmmse, *Op. Cit.*, pp. 47-48)

[3] Julius Clausen, in Kirmmse, *Op. Cit.*, p. 54.

[4] Bretall, *Op. Cit.*, p. 20.

ideal of a "both-and" synthesis, which reconciles conflicting ideas. For Kierkegaard, living involves making choices between mutually exclusive alternatives, the most important of which — the choice of how to ultimately justify one's life — determines the entire course and meaning of one's life.

The publication of *Either/Or* caused quite a sensation:

> A new literary comet...has soared in the heavens here — a harbinger and a bringer of bad fortune. It is so demonic that one reads and reads it, puts it aside in dissatisfaction, but always takes it up again, because one can neither let it go nor hold onto it. "But what is it?" I can hear you say. It is *Either/Or* by Søren Kierkegaard. You have no idea what a sensation it has caused. I think that no book has caused such a stir with the reading public since Rousseau placed his *Confessions* on the altar.[1]

Starting with *Either/Or*, Kierkegaard began the practice of alternating writing books using a pseudonym (although everyone knew that Kierkegaard was the author[2]) with works published under his own name. It is generally believed that he took responsibility for the works published under his own name in a different sense — they involved "direct communication" by Kierkegaard as a "whole man" — whereas the more popular works written using a pseudonym involved "indirect communication" and only partial truths, what could be said looking at life from a particular limited perspective. Of the pseudonymous works, O.P. Sturzen-Becker, a Swedish author who lived in Copenhagen from 1844-47 and who himself wrote under a pseudonym, said:

> One month he has the name "Johannes de Silentio," another month "Constantin Constantius," next "Vigilius Hafniensis," then "Nicolaus Notabene," "Johannes Climacus," and "Hilarius Bookbinder." All these works could really be viewed as speculative fantasies of a sort....Kierkegaard himself calls them "thought experiments," his favorite term and, with a truly remarkable talent, he discusses almost everything in the world at once — topics of a metaphysical

---

[1] Letter from Signe Læssøe to Hans Christian Andersen, April, 1843, quoted in Kirmmse, *Op. Cit.*, p. 57.

[2] He sometimes gave his own name as the editor.

10

nature as well as aesthetic, psychological, and social themes — holding it all together by means of the bass melody provided by dialectics as well as the incessant piping of "Socratic irony." In truth, Kierkegaard is the [Johann] Sebastian Bach of dialectics.[1]

In quick succession, six more major pseudonymous works appeared after *Either/Or* — *Repetition* (1843), *Fear and Trembling* (1843), *The Concept of Anxiety* (1844), *Philosophical Fragments* (1844), *Stages on Life's Way* (1845) and the massive *Concluding Unscientific Postscript* (1846) which, ironically, was supposed to be an addendum to the brief *Philosophical Fragments* — in addition to many sermon-like "edifying" discourses published under Kierkegaard's own name.

In the well-known works *Fear and Trembling* and *Concluding Unscientific Postscript*, Kierkegaard presented a very unorthodox, at times even shocking, view of Christianity which he maintained is irrational, distinct from the ethical, and where doctrines are not important. Furthermore, becoming a Christian is not an activity one can do with others (thus dispensing with organized religion) and, although open to all, it's incredibly rare to find a true believer.

Kierkegaard lived alone, attended by a manservant, never inviting people into his home[2] But, since it was important for him to study human nature, he spent his days walking about town, finding people to talk to.[3] Kierkegaard would take people by the arm and follow along with them.[4] He enjoyed talking to "people of every age and every walk of life"[5]: "He would engage himself with anyone and everyone, just as accessible to everyone on the street as he was inaccessible in his home."[6] Occasionally he took carriage rides in the forests around Copenhagen. He would write in the evenings. Meir Aron Goldschmidt,

---

[1] Quoted in Kirmmse, *Op. Cit.*, p. 93.

[2] "He who writes for 'that single individual' lives alone, inaccessible and, when all is said and done, known by no one." (Frederikke Bremer, in Kirmmse, *Op. Cit.*, pp. 94-5)

[3] "The fact is *he walks about town all day*, and generally in some person's company; only in the evening does he write and read." (Andrew Hamilton, in Kirmmse, *Op. Cit.*, p. 96)

[4] Vilhelm Birkedal, in Kirmmse, *Op. Cit.*, p. 106.

[5] Tycho E. Spang, in Kirmmse, *Op. Cit.*, p. 111.

[6] Georg Brandes, in Kirmmse, *Op. Cit.*, p. 98.

who later attacked Kierkegaard in *The Corsair*, described the impression Kierkegaard made on others:

> He looked like a person who was elevated above many or most of the ordinary conditions and temptations of life, though not in such a way that he seemed enviable or happy. The shape of his body was striking, not really ugly, certainly not repulsive, but with something disharmonious, rather slight, and yet also weighty. He went about like a thought that had got distracted at the very moment at which it was formed....There was a sort of unreality about him....for myself and for the others who saw him "in his salon on the street," he was the sort of person to whom one could tell one's sorrows, not in order for him to feel them and share them but in order for him to investigate them. The result would nonetheless be a certain comfort, because his "unreality" was not so much dead cold or stone cold but was the coolness of the higher regions, of the starry heavens. Very often he was superior and ironic...but one also felt that there was a vast background that justified it.[1]

During the early part of this period, C. J. Brandt, a pastor and historian of Danish literature, reported having had a conversation with Kierkegaard in which Kierkegaard stated that:

> He had come to the conclusion that from now on he was going to read only "writings by men who have been executed." Strange as it sounds, it is nonetheless based on the truth that there is something to be learned only from those who have offered their lives for their convictions. At the time it sounded so paradoxical to me that I was compelled to laugh. Now I am annoyed with myself for not having pursued the ironist into more serious territory.[2]

Two points can be made about this conversation: (1) Kierkegaard believed that it is of utmost importance that people really *live* by their beliefs and that means being prepared to make sacrifices for them (as he had sacrificed his love for Regine) — even the ultimate sacrifice of

---

[1] Quoted in Kirmmse, *Op. Cit.*, pp. 84-5.
[2] C.J. Brandt, September 1, 1843, quoted in Kirmmse, *Op. Cit.*, p. 59.

death. So only the words of people who are prepared to die for their beliefs are worth reading. What people say or write which is not supported by actions are mere words. (2) Kierkegaard was typically not understood by those around him.[1] It took time for his profound thoughts to find a receptive audience — about a century for the world of Philosophy to discover and fully appreciate him[2]: "If this generation will not listen to my words, there will come another one after this, which perhaps will."[3]

In 1846, during *The Corsair* incident[4], Kierkegaard published *The Present Age: A Literary Review*, ostensively a review of the now forgotten novel *The Two Ages*, but really a social critique of the times in which he lived —"an age which [was] without passion." In *The Present Age*, Kierkegaard condemned the rule of "the public," an "abstraction" which is "the most dangerous of all powers and the most insignificant" in that it is "less than a single real man, no matter how unimportant." The chief spokesman of the public is the press, according to Kierkegaard, which by its very nature appeals to humanity's lowest common denominator.

In March of 1847, Kierkegaard published *Edifying Discourses in Various Spirits*, which included *Purity of Heart is to Will One Thing*, one of his central themes, and also emphasized individualism and was strongly critical of the ecclesiastical and political tendencies of his day. *Works of Love* was published later that same year and *Two Minor Ethico-Religious Essays* were written in 1847, but not published until 1849. *Christian Discourses, The Sickness Unto Death* and *Training in Christianity* were all written in 1848[5], at a time when the revolution in Paris led to the conservative establishment in Denmark being replaced

---

[1] His works were "pretty much inaccessible to the general public," according to Sturzen-Becker.

[2] Of course part of the problem was that he wrote in a minor language.

[3] Kierkegaard in conversation with Niels Johansen, in Kirmmse, *Op. Cit.*, p. 114.

[4] *The Corsair* incident began with an article, critical of *The Corsair,* by Kierkegaard that was published by *Fædrelandet* on December 27, 1845. In January 1846 *The Corsair*'s editor, M.A. Goldschmidt and others "began to tease, parody, and caricature Kierkegaard; this lasted about six months." (Kirmmse, *Op. Cit.*, p. 334)

[5] In his *Journal* he said that 1848 was "incomparably the richest and most fruitful year I have experienced as an author." (Bretall, *Op. Cit.*, p. 339)

by a more liberal order, resulting in instituting a parliamentary government.

The Sickness Unto Death, one of Kierkegaard's greatest works, explored the realm of the subconscious fifty years before Freud. In it Kierkegaard argued that, from a religious perspective,

> Every human existence which is not conscious of itself as spirit, or conscious of itself before God as spirit...whatever it accomplishes, though it be the most amazing exploit, whatever it explains, though it were the whole of existence, however intensely it enjoys life aesthetically — every such existence is after all despair.[1]

This despair is a sickness of the self. It is worse than the worst physical ailment because "even the last hope, death, is not available." The despairing man cannot die because despair cannot "consume the eternal thing, the self, which is the ground of despair." The solution is "to will to be that self which one truly is," acknowledging the eternal part of oneself and its author, God.

Kierkegaard began to set the stage for his "attack on Christendom" with *Training in Christianity*, which he did not publish until 1850. Next came several autobiographical pieces. In *The Point of View for My Activity as an Author*, which Kierkegaard elected not to publish because he thought it too personal, Kierkegaard returned to a theme of egalitarian individualism and the fundamental problem with organized religion, which must emphasize the group and not the individual: "every individual in the race (not an outstanding individual, but every individual) is greater than the race. This is inherent in the God-relationship — and it is Christianity whose category is the individual...[2] In *On My Activity as an Author* (published in 1851), Kierkegaard explained the difference between his approach to Christianity and the Church's. Bruce H. Kirmmse summarized it in this way:

> According to SK, the traditional tactic has been to get as many people as possible to subscribe to Christianity, even if one were not sure that it really was Christianity to which they

---

[1] *The Sickness Unto Death*, in Bretall, *Op. Cit.*, p. 348.

[2] Quoted in Kirmmse, *Kierkegaard in Golden Age Denmark*, Indiana University Press, Bloomington, Ind., 1990, p. 409.

were subscribing. SK's tactic, he explains, has been to state "Christianity's requirement" to its "full ideality," even if it should prove so lofty that not a single person could accept it. His tactic has not been to provide an "apology" for Christianity but to prepare *us* for an apologizing or humiliating confession when we dare to call ourselves Christians.[1]

The official Church of Denmark remained silent to Kierkegaard's plea for honesty about how far it was from true Christianity. Instead, the Church began ingratiating itself with the new liberal democratic forces. Kierkegaard chose not to publish anything for over three years, from September, 1851 to December, 1854. He was running low on funds (he paid his own publication costs); but, more importantly, he was waiting for the venerable Bishop Mynster, the primate of all Denmark, a man who had greatly impressed Kierkegaard's father, to die (he died on January 30, 1854) and the fall of the extremely conservative A.S. Ørsted ministry which was then in power (it fell in December of 1854).

In December of 1854, Kierkegaard began his long-contemplated "attack on Christendom." There were two phases to the attack[2]: (1) "the *Fatherland* phase" (December, 1854 - May, 1855), consisting of a series of articles in that newspaper which began with a continuing call for an "admission" from the Church that the official Christianity of Denmark was not the Christianity of the New Testament and culminated in a call for a complete boycott of all official ecclesiastical activities:

> Whoever you are, whatever your life might be, my friend, by ceasing to participate (if you do) in public worship as it presently is (with its claim to being the Christianity of the New Testament) you will continually have one sin fewer, and a great sin: You are not taking part in making a fool of God.[3]

(2) "*The Moment* phase" (May 1855 until his death), consisting of articles he published himself in the magazine he created which had

---

[1] Kirmmse, *Op. Cit.*, p. 408.
[2] See Kirmmse, *Op. Cit.*, p. 451.
[3] Quoted in Kirmmse, *Op. Cit.*, p. 462.

quite a wide circulation, in which he finally called for a complete separation of Church and State, a radical view at the time.

In one issue of *The Moment*, in a statement intended to be reminiscent of Socrates[1], Kierkegaard admitted that he himself was not a Christian — something he had said many years before, using a pseudonym, in *Fear and Trembling* — but neither was anyone else, and at least he knew that he was not:

> I am not a Christian, and unfortunately I can make it apparent that the others are not either — indeed, that they are even less so than I. This is because they imagine themselves to be, or they lie their way into being it [Christian]....The only analogy I hold before myself is Socrates. My task is a Socratic task, to revise the definition of being Christian. I myself do not call myself a Christian (keeping the ideal free), but I can make it apparent that the others are even less so.[2]

Kierkegaard claimed that, unlike being a genius, which is rare, everyone *could* become a Christian; however, in fact, it occurs more rarely than genius.

In another issue of *The Moment*, Kierkegaard maintained that human beings — who desire comfortable, natural lives — have employed "perjurers" (priests) to render Christianity — which is unnatural and uncomfortable — innocuous and more palatable. They are too afraid to reject Christianity outright, which would be more honest.[3]

> This is "the priest's" significance to society, which from generation to generation consumes a "necessary" quota of perjurers in order, under the name of Christianity, to be

---

[1] Socrates had claimed, when an oracle said that he was the wisest of all men, that he didn't know anything himself; but, unlike others who thought they knew something when they didn't (Socrates spent his life questioning others to determine this), he at least knew that he didn't know anything, so perhaps he was wiser than they were.

[2] Quoted in Kirmmse, *Op. Cit.*, p. 464.

[3] "The difference between the freethinker and official Christianity is that the freethinker is an honest man who straightforwardly *teaches* that Christianity is poetry, fiction. Official Christianity is a falsification...." (Quoted in Kirmmse, *Op. Cit.*, p. 470)

completely secured against Christianity, to be completely secure in being able to live in heathendom, safe, and even refined by the fact that this is Christianity.[1]

The State exists to make sure that all that people need is easily available to them, so why not "eternal blessedness" as well![2] Secondarily, the clergy's function is to also authorize socially useful activities — "The Christianity of 'the priests' addresses itself to using religion (which exists for precisely the opposite purpose) to cement families together"[3] — like infant baptism and confirmation.

In the final issue of *The Moment*, Kierkegaard accused the clergy of encouraging people's natural desire to avoid taking responsibility for their lives, when they should be doing just the opposite, because Christianity is all about individual responsibility:

> All "humanity's" shrewdness is directed toward one thing, toward being able to live without responsibility. The significance of the priest for society ought to be to do everything to make every person eternally responsible for every hour that he lives, even in the least things he does, because this is Christianity. But, his significance for society is to guarantee hypocrisy, while society pushes off the responsibility from itself onto "the priest."[4]

On October 2, 1855, Kierkegaard collapsed on the street and was taken to Frederik's Hospital, terminally ill with "paralysis of the legs as a consequence of tuberculosis of the spine marrow."[5] Two weeks later, close friend Emil Boesen, who visited him in the hospital, asked him if there was anything he still wanted to say. Kierkegaard replied:

> No. Yes, greet everyone for me. I have liked them all very much, and tell them that my life is a great suffering, unknown and inexplicable to other people. Everything looked like pride and vanity, but it wasn't. I am absolutely no better than other people, and I have said so and have never said anything else. I

---

[1] In Kirmmse, *Op. Cit.*, p. 471.

[2] See Kirmmse, *Op. Cit.*, p. 474.

[3] *Ibid.*, p. 472.

[4] *Ibid.*, p. 471-2.

[5] Hansine Andræ, in Kirmmse, *Encounters with Kierkegaard*, p. 118.

have had my thorn in the flesh, and therefore I did not marry and could not accept an official [ecclesiastical] position....I think I have had a task that was sufficient!y appropriate, important and difficult. You must take note of the fact that I have seen things from within the innermost center of Christianity...."[1]

Towards the end, young Troels Frederick Troel-Lund who, although not a blood relative, was related to Kierkegaard by marriage, visited him in the hospital in the company of relatives. He was profoundly affected by the last moments he had with Kierkegaard:

> When I extended my hand to him, the others had already turned toward the door, so it was as though we were alone. He took my hand in both of his own — how small, thin, and transparently white they were — and said only: "Thank you for coming to see me Troels! And now live well!" But these ordinary words were accompanied by a look of which I have never since seen the equal. It radiated with an elevated, transfigured, blessed brilliance, so that it seemed to me to illuminate the entire room. Everything was concentrated in the flood of light from those eyes: profound love, beatifically dissolved sadness, an all-penetrating clarity, and a playful smile. For me it was like a heavenly revelation, an emanation from one soul to another, a blessing, which infused me with new courage, strength, and responsibility.[2]

Kierkegaard died the evening of November 11, 1855, finally obtaining "the peace for which he had so deeply longed."[3]

How to handle his burial created a problem for Kierkegaard's family:

> There were two alternatives. Either to let it take place in the quietest possible way or to proceed in the usual way. By permitting it to take place quietly — i.e., in a clandestine and secret fashion — one would appear to dishonor the deceased, appear to take sides and to declare his life's work (which

---

[1] In Kirmmse, *Op. Cit.*, pp. 124-5.
[2] Troels Frederik Troels-Lund, in Kirmmse, *Op. Cit.*, p. 190.
[3] *Ibid.*

everyone was talking about at the time) as best served by silence and oblivion. On the other hand, by permitting it to take place in accordance with the usual forms — starting from a church, with a eulogy by a clergyman, etc. — one would strike a strongly discordant note, because everyone knew that the deceased had characterized pastors as "liars, deceivers, perjurers; quite literally, without exception, not one honest pastor."[1]

The decision was made by Kierkegaard's brother, Peter Christian Kierkegaard, a parish pastor, who chose the second course and gave the eulogy himself. Crowds of people showed up and "a great scandal occurred at the grave"[2] when Henrik Lund, Kierkegaard's nephew, a medical resident who had attended to Kierkegaard in the hospital, denounced the hypocritical event and claimed that it showed that Kierkegaard was right in his assessment of the Church. He ended his speech with these words:

> ...both on his behalf and on my own, I protest viewing our presence here as participation in the worship of God sponsored by "official Christianity," because he has been brought here against his repeatedly expressed will, and has in a way been violated. And I have come along only in order to ascertain what has now taken place. In any other case, after having understood what "official Christianity" is, neither I nor he would have been present at any "officially Christian" action.
> I have spoken and freed my spirit![3]

Even in death, Kierkegaard was at the center of controversy. He would have liked that.

Thus ended the life of a man who led a deceptively uneventful existence, conversing amicably in the streets with others by day and writing alone at home at night, expressing profound thoughts that challenged almost every view society held dear and which revealed a

---

[1] *Ibid.*, pp. 190-1.
[2] Letter from Hans Lassen Martensen to L. Gude, November 18, 1855, quoted in Kirmmse, *Op. Cit.*, p. 135.
[3] Quoted in Kirmmse, *Op. Cit.*, p. 135.

depth of reflection about life seldom found in this world — thoughts which few were ready to hear.

> That was how he lived: walking, riding in carriages, conversing and above all writing, always writing. With the help of his pen he conversed not only with his times but with himself. In few human lives has ink played so large a role. At his death he left about thirty printed volumes, which taken together constitute almost (as he called it) a literature within literature, and he left equally many large volumes of handwritten journals. And almost all of this was written during the final twelve years of his life. Such was the odd and drab external appearance of the life of one of the most inwardly agitated lives that has ever been lived here in Denmark.[1]

---

[1] Georg Brandes, in Kirmmse, *Op. Cit.*, p. 98.

II

Kierkegaard's Philosophy

[Kierkegaard's] appeal is ever to the living individual, the solitary, concerned individual who, not unmindful of his eternal destiny, seeks an absolute direction for his life amid the relativities of time. To such a one Kierkegaard speaks — indirectly at first, then directly and with mounting eloquence. And such a one can hardly fail to listen.- Robert Bretall[1]

Introduction

Anyone who attempts to sum up the philosophy of Søren Kierkegaard must be concerned about at least three things: (1) He did not give his own name as the author of most of his works, particularly those which have made him famous. His use of fictional pseudonymous authors suggests that the "truths" contained in these works are not necessarily Kierkegaard's own beliefs. Instead, the consensus of opinion is that these works most likely give us "truths" about life as viewed only from a particular, limited perspective. (2) Kierkegaard was not a systematic philosopher. He was rebelling against "systems". We can see that (1) and (2) are connected, because the use of pseudonymous authors for his works is entirely appropriate

---

[1] Bretall, *Op. Cit.*, pp. xxiv-xxv.

for someone who believes that there is no single "correct" perspective on life. (3) Finally, as Henry E. Allison states:

> Kierkegaard remains perpetually elusive. Like Socrates, of whom he was a life long admirer, he believed that his task was not to expound but to sting....[1]

Does this mean that there is no overall philosophy contained in Kierkegaard's works? To the contrary, I believe that an overall philosophy can be inferred from piecing the different perspectives together. Furthermore, I think that in his writings we can find common truths which indicate the "big picture" as Kierkegaard sees it. Certain themes are repeatedly emphasized. To understand what Kierkegaard means by "truth is subjectivity," "either/or," the aesthetic, ethical and religious spheres of existence, faith, "purity of heart," passion, and the "chief thing in life": "to win yourself, acquire your own self" will enable us to grasp Kierkegaard's philosophy. Although he does not tell us how we should live our lives, Kierkegaard does lay out the options, describe what is involved in making the choice, and explain why it is crucial that we choose for ourselves and in time. Kierkegaard demands more of his readers than most philosophers. This is not because his "truths" are so difficult to grasp; but because, according to his own philosophy, they don't mean anything unless his readers have taken them up into their own lives. In his method, again, the comparison is made to Socrates:

> Like Socrates, Kierkegaard is also a kind of gadfly who stings his audience until it performs the essential act of introspective self-knowledge. But it is you, the reader, who must do the essential work....[2]

I should warn the reader that, in what follows, I shall be giving a sympathetic presentation of Kierkegaard's philosophy. It will be sympathetic in three respects: First, I shall use the "principle of

---

[1] "Christianity and Nonsense," in *Kierkegaard: A Collection of Critical Essays*, Edited by Josiah Thompson, Doubleday & Company, Inc., Garden City, New York, 1972, p. 323.

[2] Henry D. Aiken, *The Age of Ideology*, Chapter XI, "The Advent of Existentialism: Søren Kierkegaard," New American Library, New York, 1956, p. 226.

charitable interpretation" whenever possible to attempt to show that Kierkegaard's overall philosophy can be summarized in such a way that it is both consistent and plausible. There will be textual purists who will be unhappy with this approach, but I am more interested in finding what is worthwhile in Kierkegaard's philosophy than in finding things to quibble with. Second, Kierkegaard, like most (if not all) philosophers, was a product of his times; he was reacting to what was going on during the first half of the nineteenth century, particularly in his own country of Denmark. I am going to resist, however, giving the narrowest possible reading of his works, as reactions to particular conditions that have ceased to exist, which would make it questionable whether he has something to say to us at the turn of the twenty-first century. I will consistently attempt to give the broadest possible interpretation of Kierkegaard's main ideas because, as is true with all *great* philosophers, I believe that he has much to say to us today. Finally, I should confess that each time I return to reading Kierkegaard, I find myself more and more impressed. I would like to convince you, the reader, of Kierkegaard's greatness. This is the primary task I have set myself.

It is appropriate to begin a discussion of Kierkegaard's philosophy by indicating what he was reacting against in his day, because it will help us to get clearer about some of his own ideas. This may seem at odds with my intention to show that Kierkegaard's philosophy can be summarized in such a way that transcends the particular concerns he had about the state of Philosophy, Christianity and culture in the early nineteenth century. I believe, however, that there is a tendency, in any age, for people to hold the views which he found so objectionable in his own day.

23

What Kierkegaard was Reacting Against

Let us start with a brief summary of the philosophy of Georg Wilhelm Friedrich Hegel (1770-1831), whose intellectual legacy "weighed heavily on the living" in the nineteenth century, as Marx was to later say, and give Kierkegaard's reaction to it.

Hegel

There are five important ideas in Hegel's mature work (see particularly *The Phenomenology of Spirit*, 1807), which form the basis of the Hegelian system: (1) His belief that Philosophy should be *scientific*, that is objective, rational and systematic. (2) His notion of *Geist* (translated as "Spirit" or "Mind" and also referred to as "The Truth," "The Absolute" and "The Idea") which is equivalent to the Divine and is in all of us. Hegel replaces the idea of a transcendent God, a being who is distinct from human beings and from whom we would then feel alienated, with an immanent God, who is one with human consciousness. Many Hegelian scholars believe that his notion of "Geist" is derived from Kant's "transcendental ego," the "real" self that can't be perceived but only argued to as a presupposition for one's being able to have experiences at all. Kant's notion of "transcendental ego," without the possibility of individuation — since it lies in the noumenal world and thus the categories of the Understanding (including unity and plurality) don't apply to it — thought of as divine seems to be Hegel's notion of "Geist." (3) His view of *history* as not simply a chronology of events, but also representing *progress*. History has a purpose which is the gradual recognition of *Geist*. Hegel viewed the present as the end-product, or goal, of the past. The task of Philosophy is to rationalize the present in terms of the past. (4) Hegel's *dialectic* where history moves from one stage, to a conflicting stage, and then to a third stage which *synthesizes* the previous two stages, that is, preserves what is true in the previous two stages. (5) Hegel's conception of *freedom* which is very different from the popular conception of freedom as the ability to do as one pleases. Instead, for Hegel, freedom is the power to "realize oneself," which involves recognizing one's membership in the historically evolving community. Ultimately, the free person is the one who is able to identify him/herself with the duties and responsibilities of the

Prussian-Christian State which, for Hegel, is *Geist* objectified and a complete synthesis of human beings in their particularity with human beings in their universality.

Kierkegaard rejects each one of these views: (1) The emphasis on the rational and the search for objective truth, which had heretofore dominated Western Philosophy and reached its culmination in the Hegelian system, doesn't appreciate the limitations of reason and objectivity.

> ...the thing is to find a truth which is true *for me*, to find *the idea for which I can live and die*. What would be the use of discovering so-called objective truth, of working through all the systems of philosophy and of being able, if required, to review them all and show up the inconsistencies within each system; what good would it do me to be able to develop a theory of the state and combine all the details into a single whole, and so construct a world in which I did not live, but only held up to the view of others...what good would it do me if truth stood before me, cold and naked, not caring whether I recognized her or not...? I certainly do not deny that I still recognize an *imperative of understanding* and that through it one can work upon men, *but it must be taken up into my life*, and that is what I now recognize as the most important thing. That is what my soul longs after, as the African desert thirsts for water.[1]

According to Kierkegaard, what is needed for action, for finding the thing "for which [you] can live and die," is not reason and objectivity, but *passion* and *subjectivity*. The search for a rational, objective philosophy might be intellectually stimulating, but it won't help you to live: "Usually the philosophers (Hegel as well as the rest), like the majority of men, exist in quite different categories for everyday purposes from those in which they speculate."[2] Kierkegaard demands of Philosophy that it advise us on how to *live*.

(2) The individual is eliminated altogether in Hegel's theory of *Geist*, a universal consciousness. In Hegel's view, individuals are essentially representatives of their age. There is no place for individuals

---

[1] *Journal*, 1835, in Bretall, *Op. Cit.*, p. 5.

[2] *Journal*, 1835, quoted in Robert Solomon, *From Rationalism to Existentialism*, Harper and Row, New York, 1972, p. 78.

with particular thoughts and feelings, for the *subjective* viewpoint, which is what Kierkegaard is concerned with.

> For Kierkegaard, Hegel's much vaunted historical consciousness is not a way of coming to more complete understanding of one's own condition as an existing being, but essentially an escape from it....all Hegel really accomplished was to absorb the individual's particular existence into that abstraction to end all abstractions, the Absolute, in which every remaining vestige of concrete existence is finally lost.[1]

Also, by reducing God to *Geist*, eliminating any distance between human beings and God, Hegel is attempting to make it too easy to be religious.

(3) Hegel's backward-looking, historical evolutionary view ignores the living human being who must make decisions, who must act alone, *now*: "It is perfectly true, as philosophers say, that life must be understood backwards. But they forget the other proposition, that it must be lived forwards."[2]

(4) Hegel's claim that apparently contradictory views can, and should, be synthesized is fundamentally opposed to Kierkegaard's belief that life consists of making "either/or" choices. In particular, according to Kierkegaard, the individual must make a choice between three mutually exclusive ways of living one's life.

(5) Kierkegaard strongly disagrees with Hegel's notion of "positive" freedom — which he wouldn't consider to be freedom at all — where individuals assert their freedom by conforming to the rational ideals of their age. According to Kierkegaard, this amounts to trying to escape taking responsibility for one's actions, something which Kierkegaard's emphasis on individual freedom will not permit.

Previous Views Concerning What is Necessary to be Religious

Before Kierkegaard it was thought, by philosophers and theologians, that to believe in God one must be convinced that the doctrines of one's religion are rationally defensible. Along these lines,

---

[1] Aiken, *Op. Cit.*, pp. 226-7.
[2] *Journal*, 1843, in Solomon, *Op. Cit.*, p. 78.

there were many proofs for the existence of God[1] and attempts to show that there are solutions to the Problem of Evil and other apparent problems in reconciling God's attributes either with each other or with the existence of the world as we find it. In a slightly different move, but still an attempt to rationally justify believing in God, Kant had argued that the central doctrines of religion must be accepted as presuppositions for morality.[2]

Ordinary people were encouraged, by religious leaders, to believe that they were automatically members of the religion of their parents. Perhaps they had to go through a symbolic ritual such as, for Christians, being baptized. In a country like Kierkegaard's Denmark in the early nineteenth century, where there was no separation of Church and State, one could consider oneself a Christian just by living in that country.

Kierkegaard strongly objected to the attempts to make it rational and easy to be religious, in particular to be a Christian. In his view, not only was it not rational to believe in God, it was positively *irrational*. Furthermore, this characteristic of religious belief was not thought by him to be a weakness, but a strength, because it made *faith* possible. Kierkegaard believed that far from being easy to truly believe in God, as opposed to just paying lip service to a belief in God, it was the hardest thing in the world. Yet we all have the capacity to become true believers and, according to Kierkegaard, it is worth the effort.

Kierkegaard also rejected the central premise of organized religion, that being religious is a group activity. According to Kierkegaard, becoming religious involves establishing a one-to-one relationship with God and no one else can help you do this. Attending some sort of religious service with others will not automatically make you religious.

---

[1] Most notably the Ontological, Cosmological and Teleological Proofs.

[2] Kant's argument essentially went like this: We must be moral, we recognize the validity of the Categorical Imperative; but realistically we know that our good behavior will not necessarily be rewarded in *this* life. In order for our being moral to make sense, there must be an eventual uniting of virtue and happiness, an ultimate reward for the virtuous (the *summum bonum*). There must, therefore, be a God and an afterlife in which God rewards or punishes us according to our behavior in this life.

"The Present Age"

Besides being guilty of watering down religion to make it easier to believe in God, Kierkegaard also criticized the age in which he lived for lacking in *passion*. People were reflective enough, perhaps too reflective. There is a danger that too much reflection, too much emphasis on abstract thought, can lead to a paralysis of the will: "Do it, or don't do it — you will regret both."[1] According to Kierkegaard, we have to act, we have to make choices, without having a guarantee that we're doing the right thing. There isn't a single right way to behave; there's only *what's right for you*, and you're the only judge of that. Deciding how to live is not an intellectual choice, it requires passionately committing to something, and what's at stake is one's very identity as a person.

Kierkegaard was also critical of conformist tendencies in his day, of people uniformly banding together, discouraging individuals from taking risks on their own. "The Public" was winning its battle against "the Individual" and the Press, which appeals to the lowest common denominator, was its primary instrument in waging this war. The problem with being part of "the Public," an abstraction according to Kierkegaard, is that "[n]o single person who belongs to the public makes a real commitment."[2] There is much power in the Public and yet it is a "nothing." One must dare to be an individual, for it is only in doing so that one can lead a meaningful life.

The Tendencies in Any Age

I believe that what Kierkegaard was criticizing in Hegel's philosophy and in the attitudes of his own age are general tendencies in *any* age. In any age, people tend to identify with the collective, to see themselves as just a product of their time and place, because it allows them to escape taking personal responsibility for their own actions: "even more than death the individual fears...risk[ing] something on his own."[3] In any age, people are afraid to make a passionate commitment to anything, particularly without guarantees. In any age, there is a

---

[1] *Either/Or, Vol. II: Equilibrium Between the Aesthetical and the Ethical in the Composition of Personality*, in Bretall, *Op. Cit.*, p. 98.

[2] *The Present Age*, quoted in Bretall, *Op. Cit.*, p. 266.

[3] *The Present Age*, in Bretall, *Op. Cit.*, p. 261.

tendency to reduce people to the lowest common denominator, to discourage greatness and uniqueness. The "sorry and ludicrous condition of the majority of men" is "that in their own house they prefer to live in the cellar."[1] In any age, people want the comfort religion can bring, without exerting any effort:

> ...the bourgeois' love of God begins when vegetable life is most active, when the hands are comfortably folded on the stomach, and the head sinks back into the cushions of the chair, while the eyes, drunk with sleep, gaze heavily for a moment towards the ceiling.[2]

People want, fundamentally, an easy, secure life.

The problem with all of this, in Kierkegaard's eyes, is that it doesn't recognize the true human predicament; and the danger in living an easy life as part of "the Public" is that one will have missed the boat entirely. Even though you might have impressed others, you will have lost your own self, the only important thing in life. There will come a "midnight hour" when you will realize this, but then it may be too late to do anything about it.

---

[1] *The Sickness Unto Death*, quoted in Bretall, *Op. Cit.*, p.346.

[2] *Journal*, 1837, in Bretall, *Op. Cit.*, p. 9.

Study Question

1. What was Kierkegaard reacting against in developing his philosophy? Do you think that the concerns he had about the tendencies of people living in his own age apply to people living today?

The Main Themes in Kierkegaard's Philosophy

We're now ready to turn to an examination of the major themes in Kierkegaard's philosophy: (1) Individualism, (2) "Truth is Subjectivity," (3) "Either/Or," (4) Three Spheres of Existence, (5) Faith, (6) "Purity of Heart," (7) Passion, and (8) The "chief thing in life": "to win yourself, acquire your own self."

Individualism

> Had I to carve an inscription on my grave I would ask for none other than "the individual."[1]

> The man who can really stand alone in the world, only taking counsel from his own conscience — that man is a hero....[2]

Above all else, what can be said of Kierkegaard is that he is an individualist. For Kierkegaard the only important entity is the "existing individual" and all his writings were intended to try to help the existing individual lead a meaningful, fulfilled life. Kierkegaard denies the possibility of a collective, social solution to the problem of how to live one's life. Each solitary individual must choose, and follow, his or her own path.

To understand what it means to say that Kierkegaard is an individualist, it is important to distinguish between two views which are often confused with one another: Individualism and Ethical Egoism. One reason they are thought to be equivalent is that they each claim to have Collectivism as its opposite. There are two different senses of Collectivism, however, which I shall call Collectivism$_1$ and Collectivism$_2$, that have Individualism and Ethical Egoism, respectively, as their opposites.

The debate between Individualism and Collectivism$_1$ concerns whether the fundamental unit, when discussing the category of human beings, is the particular individual human being or persons in groups.

---

[1] *Journal*, in Bretall, *Op. Cit.*, p. 258.
[2] *Journal*, early 1850's, in Bretall, *Op. Cit.*, p. 429.

Sociologists would seem to hold the latter view, that it is wrong to focus on particular individuals because we are essentially social beings: "we did not create ourselves,...we owe what we are to the communities that formed us...."[1] According to this view, we are a product of social conditioning and so it makes no sense to talk about us as separate individuals, except secondarily as embodiments of the views — including the ethical values — of the societies of which we are members. Individualists, on the other hand, claim that we are able to, and must, choose as individuals how to live our lives, including choosing the values we shall live by. We can choose to accept the values of a particular group or not. What the distinction, then, comes down to is whether value is relative to individuals or groups.

It should be clear, from my earlier discussion of Hegel's philosophy, that he was a collectivist in the sense of Collectivism₁ and that Kierkegaard rejects this view. In Hegel's philosophy:

> Being an individual man is a thing that has been abolished, and every speculative philosopher confuses himself with humanity at large, whereby he becomes something infinitely great — and at the same time nothing at all.[2]

In real life, according to Kierkegaard, there is no such thing as a collective human being. There are only individual human beings.

The distinction between Ethical Egoism and Collectivism₂ does not concern whether value is relative to individuals or groups, that is, whether individuals can choose their own values or not. The issue, instead, becomes one of *what our values should be*. According to Ethical Egoism, one should always act in a self-interested manner. A collectivist₂, on the other hand, believes that one should act in the manner which would be best for the group. As we shall see, Kierkegaard believes that accepting the view of Ethical Egoism is *one* option for how an individual can live his or her life and Collectivism₂ represents another option. (Neither one is the option which he personally chose.) The fact that, according to Kierkegaard, *individuals* are faced with these options in life, that we can each choose different

---

[1] R. Bellah, R. Madsen, W. Sullivan, A. Swindler, and S. Tipton, *Habits of the Heart: Individualism and Commitment in American Life*, University of California Press, Berkeley, California, 1985, p. 295.
[2] *Concluding Unscientific Postscript*, in Bretall, *Op. Cit.*, p. 206.

values, shows that he is an individualist and that he rejects Collectivism₁.

The difference between Individualism and Ethical Egoism can now be stated fairly succinctly: According to Individualism, individuals choose their own values and they *may* choose to act in a self-interested manner, but then again they may not. According to Ethical Egoism, one *should* act in a self-interested manner. Similarly, the difference between Collectivism₁ and Collectivism₂ is that Collectivism₁ is the view that values are chosen collectively and the collective *may* choose to require individuals to sacrifice their own interests for the group, although it doesn't have to, whereas Collectivism₂ is the view that people *should* be required to act for the benefit of society as a whole.

With these distinctions in mind, it is interesting to compare Kierkegaard's position with that of another great nineteenth century philosopher, Friedrich Nietzsche, who is also said to be an individualist. Nietzsche maintained that there are two distinct types of people; he called them masters and slaves. Only the masters, who are relatively small in number, have the strength of will to be able to choose their own values. These are the strong willed, creative people — the artists in the broadest sense of the term — whom he advises to concentrate on developing their own talents and abilities to the fullest to make the most of their lives. It is this group of people that he wrote for, to free them from the chains of "absolute values" that denigrate creativity, invented by the large body of slaves to keep the naturally stronger masters in line. The slaves operate collectively, for this is their great strength. Nietzsche, then, is a partial individualist and partial collectivist₁, unlike Kierkegaard, who believes that *everyone* is capable of, and should, choose his or her own values. We can, further, say that Nietzsche advocates the particular value system of Ethical Egoism for his masters, whereas Kierkegaard doesn't particularly recommend Ethical Egoism to anyone, although it is, for him, a viable option as a guiding principle for living one's life.

Truth is Subjectivity

Subjectivity is truth, subjectivity is reality.[1]

---

[1] *Concluding Unscientific Postscript*, "The Subjective Thinker," in

When subjectivity is the truth, the conceptual determination of the truth must include an expression for the antithesis to objectivity, a memento of the fork in the road where the way swings off; this expression will also indicate the tension of the subjective inwardness. Here is such a definition of truth: *An objective uncertainty held fast in an appropriation-process of the most passionate inwardness is the truth*, the highest truth attainable for an *existing individual*.[1]

We have seen that Kierkegaard is an individualist and that this means that, for him, value is relative to the individual. There are no absolute values, no absolute truths that we all must accept concerning how we should live our lives. Instead, it is up to each individual to decide for himself or herself what is worth living and dying for.

The claim that "truth is subjectivity" sounds strange, even paradoxical, to most of us. Kierkegaard would respond that this is because we have become "demoralized" by science.[2] Science aims at discovering objective facts about the world which transcend personal feelings and opinions. The problem with science, according to Kierkegaard, is that its value is limited. No matter how successful it is, it will never tell us how we should live our lives; and yet, since the Renaissance, science has become increasingly important.

The history of modern philosophy, beginning with Descartes, has to a great extent been influenced by the scientific view of life. The central problem in philosophy from Descartes until Kant was epistemological: How can we be sure that there is an external world (a world "out there" which exists apart from our perception of it) and, assuming that there is one, exactly what is that world like? The focus was on the *external world* and our perception of it.

Immanuel Kant shifted the focus from the external world to the *subject* who perceives and acts in it. This was his "Copernican revolution" in Philosophy. However, it is really a *generic* subject which he was interested in, rather than the *individual* subject which is the focus of Kierkegaard's philosophy. Kant took the first step towards radical subjectivity, while Kierkegaard takes the final leap.

Bretall, *Op. Cit.*, p. 231.
[1] *Concluding Unscientific Postscript*, "The Subjective Truth: Inwardness, Truth is Subjectivity," in Bretall, *Op. Cit.*, p. 214.
[2] *Ibid.*, p. 212.

Kant differentiated between things as they appear to us — *phenomena* — and things-in-themselves — *noumena*. He maintained that the world we perceive, the phenomenal world, is determined by our perceptual apparatus, in particular the *forms of intuition* (we perceive things in a three-dimensional space and a two-dimensional time) and the *categories of the understanding* (the most important of which is causality: for us every event must have a cause). We cannot know the extent to which our perceptual apparatus distorts reality, so we shouldn't worry about what the noumenal world is like. Kant, therefore, threw out the question which was so important from Descartes on: How do we know whether the things which we experience, the phenomena, conform to the things-in-themselves, the noumena? Instead, Kant said that we should think of the forms of intuition and the categories of the understanding as defining what is a possible experience for us.

Kant gave us a radically new conception of mind, one in which mind actively forms that which it experiences. This was a very different conception of mind from Locke's conception of mind as a "blank slate" which experience writes upon. With the shift from a relatively passive self, at least with regards to perception, to a more active self, a self which determines to a large extent what it experiences, the stage was set for Kierkegaard's move to individual subjectivity.

There are two important differences between Kant and Kierkegaard with regard to the issue of subjectivity. First, Kant's forms of intuition and categories of the understanding were features of *all* human beings, so any bias in perception and understanding of the world arising from them was shared by all equally. It wasn't the case that one person perceived the world one way, while another perceived it very differently. We share the same perceptual apparatus. This is why I say that although the focus shifted from the external world to the self which perceives it, it is a *generic* self rather than a *particular* individual self.

Second, Kant was talking about perception, the self as *knower* versus the self as *agent*, when he concluded that we couldn't have objective truths about the world. When he began to explore the presuppositions of the self as agent[1], Kant argued that there are

---

[1] Kant discussed the presuppositions of the self as knower in his *Critique of Pure Reason* and the presuppositions of the self as agent in his *Critique of Practical Reason*.

objective truths. We must all obey the Categorical Imperative, which Kant maintained is the only rational principle to follow in the realm of ethics, so there is a single correct way to behave. Kant also thought that it is necessary that we have free will, and that God and immortality exist, in order to make sense of the self as an agent who is obligated to follow the Categorical Imperative. So, although Kant made the subject more important than ever before in Philosophy, he was only interested in the subject in a general way, and it didn't lead to his entirely giving up a belief in objective truths.

As we have seen, Kierkegaard, unlike Kant, refused to speak of individuals collectively. There are only particular individual human beings who need a direction for their individual lives. According to Kierkegaard, no objective facts about the world will give *a particular individual* a reason for living his or her life in a certain way. None of Kant's "objective truths" are accepted by Kierkegaard as true for *all* human beings except that we are free to choose our own way. Consider, for example, the Categorical Imperative. Even if it is true, as Kant claimed, that it is the only rational principle to follow in the realm of ethics, why must everyone think in ethical terms? Because we ought to see that other people should count as much as we do? But that just begs the question, by assuming the correctness of the ethical perspective. Any attempt to justify adopting the ethical perspective will use reasons which presuppose that perspective.

Looking at the larger picture above and beyond the emphasis on science in modern philosophy from Descartes on, one could say that the search for objective, universal truth was the central occupation of all western philosophers before Kierkegaard. Things started to shift with Kant. However, even Kant, who maintained that we couldn't have the sort of knowledge of the external world which earlier philosophers thought we could have, argued that we could have knowledge of universal truths about the phenomenal world (that it would satisfy the forms of intuition and categories of the understanding) and some objective truths about the noumenal world (human beings have free will and should obey the Categorical Imperative, the existence of God and immortality). The focus was still, to a large extent, on *what* the person believed and whether it is true or not.

Kierkegaard maintains that this emphasis on *what* is believed is wrong because it is impossible to have the certainty about what is believed that philosophers had hoped we could have and, more importantly, it couldn't give us a reason for living anyway. Only the particular individual subject could provide that. So Kierkegaard shifts the focus from *what* is believed to the subject's *relationship* to what is believed (as he puts it, to *how* it is believed). Instead of asking whether what is believed is the truth or not, he has us ask whether the subject has the proper relationship to what he or she believes. Is this relationship "in the truth"? Has the person passionately committed to believing in it? This amounts to a shift from *objective* to *subjective truth*:

> *The objective accent falls on WHAT is said, the subjective accent on HOW it is said.*...Objectively the interest is focused merely on the thought-content, subjectively on the inwardness. At its maximum this inward "how" is the passion of the infinite, and the passion of the infinite is the truth. But the passion of the infinite is precisely subjectivity, and thus subjectivity becomes the truth....Only in subjectivity is there decision, to seek objectivity is to be in error. It is the passion of the infinite that is the decisive factor and not its content....In this manner subjectivity and the subjective "how" constitute the truth.[1]

If I have committed to something with all my being, if I have staked my entire life on it, then *it is true for me*. The truth of the *what* is not particularly important. Even if what I believe in is objectively false, it can be subjectively true:

> *When the question of the truth is raised subjectively, reflection is directed subjectively to the nature of the individual's relationship: if only the mode of this relationship is in the truth, the individual is in the truth, even if he should happen to thus be related to what is not true.*[2]

Kierkegaard's notion of subjective truth can be applied to whatever ideal the person might try to realize. Objectively speaking the ideal is uncertain and so unjustified, but it becomes subjectively true by being chosen by a subject who makes a passionate commitment to it:

---

[1] *Ibid.*
[2] *Ibid.*, p. 211.

"The truth is precisely the venture which chooses an objective uncertainty with the passion of the infinite."[1]

As an example of the contrast between the futile search for objective truth and the possibility of subjective truth, Kierkegaard discusses the difference between others' belief in, and justification for, the immortality of the soul with Socrates'. In Plato's *Phaedo*, we can see that Simmias and Cebes require objective proof, in the form of a sound argument, in order to believe in the soul's immortality; and of course, for each of the three arguments which are proposed, questions can be raised which lead to doubt. Socrates, on the other hand, is about to die, and yet he has no doubt that his soul will continue to exist after his bodily death. Why the disparity? The others approach the question of the soul's immortality as an intellectual exercise; whereas Socrates has made a commitment, staked his whole life on his conviction that the soul is immortal. On his belief

> ...he risks his entire life, he has the courage to meet death, and he has with the passion of the infinite so determined the pattern of his life that it must be found acceptable....Can any better proof be given for the immortality of the soul?....The "bit" of uncertainty that Socrates had helped him, because he himself contributed the passion of the infinite; the three proofs that the others have do not profit them at all, because they are and remain dead to spirit and enthusiasm.[2]

The part about the "bit of uncertainty" is important for Kierkegaard. It is not a bad thing that we don't have objective certainty

---

[1] *Ibid.*, p. 214.

[2] *Ibid.*, p. 213. Compare with Wittgenstein who later said:

> This in one sense must be called the firmest of all beliefs, because the man risks things on account of it which he would not do on things which are by far better established for him. (Quoted in *Philosophy of Religion, Selected Readings*, edited by William L. Rowe and William J. Wainwright, Second Edition, Harcourt, Brace Jovanovich, New York, 1973, p. 276)

38

about what we believe. Objective certainty doesn't require commitment. If I *know* something is the case, it just *is*, whether I accept it or not: "what good would it do me if truth stood before me, cold and naked, not caring whether I recognized her or not...?" With at least a bit of uncertainty, I am forced to either make a commitment or not. The commitment bridges the gap which exists between myself and the object of my belief because of the uncertainty. The greater the uncertainty, the more of a commitment is required. Whether to commit or not, the choice is mine to make.

The freedom we have to choose what we will believe, how we will justify our lives, is both exciting and, at the same time, entails an awesome, frightening responsibility. As Louis Mackey puts it, Kierkegaard is telling the reader of his works who would understand him:

> You reader! Whatever you believe, whatever you claim to know, remember in fear and trembling that you hold this faith and stake this claim solely on the strength of your own freedom to do so, with no guarantee more ultimate than your own decision, at your own risk, and on your own responsibility![1]

Many people will try to find a way to avoid taking responsibility for the decision of choosing what to believe. We have seen that this is a tendency of people living in any age. They will try to find an objective basis for their decision, postponing the decision as they consider more and more arguments. This, according to Kierkegaard, is a sign that they are shirking their responsibility:

> ...it is essential that every trace of an objective issue should be eliminated. If any such trace remains, it is at once a sign that the subject seeks to shirk something of the pain and crisis of the decision; that is, he seeks to make the problem to some degree objective....if the speaker has still another argument up his sleeve, it follows that the decision is postponed....it must be regarded as an illusion rooted in the demoralization which remains ignorant of the subjective nature of the decision, or as

---

[1] "The Loss of the World in Kierkegaard's Ethics," in *Kierkegaard, A Collection of Critical Essays*, Edited by Josiah Thompson, Doubleday & Co., Garden City, N. Y., 1972, p. 267.

an evasion springing from the disingenuousness which seeks to shirk the decision by an objective mode of approach, wherein there can in all eternity be no decision....[1]

Instead, we must accept that truth is subjectivity and make a decision, commit to something, the sooner the better.

Either/Or

The most tremendous thing which has been granted to man is: the choice, freedom. (*Journal*, 1850)

Either/or. Upon me these words have always made a deep impression, and they still do, especially when I pronounce them absolutely and without specific reference to any objects, for this use of them suggests the possibility of starting the most dreadful contrasts into action. They affect me like a magic incantation, and my soul becomes exceedingly serious, sometimes almost harrowed.[2]

We've all had the experience of finding ourselves in a situation where we have a choice of actions. This afternoon I could grade papers, clean my house or read the novel which I just picked up from the library. I feel the weight of the decision, conflicting desires pulling me in different directions, but in this case "one chooses only for the moment" and "can choose something different the next moment."[3] No matter how important the choice might seem to me today, it is not what Kierkegaard has in mind when he uses the phrase "either/or."

Kierkegaard contrasts this sort of "choosing for the moment" with "choosing absolutely," choosing the direction of one's entire life. We, unlike other entities who simply are what they are, are free to become

---

[1] *Concluding Unscientific Postscript*, "The Task of Becoming Subjective," in Bretall, *Op. Cit.*, p. 207.
[2] *Either/Or, Vol. II: Equilibrium Between the Aesthetical and the Ethical in the Composition of Personality*, in Bretall, *Op. Cit.*, p. 97.
[3] *Ibid.*, p. 105.

what we will. We can choose our own values, including how we give meaning to our lives.

This is very exciting, but at the same time frightening as well. We are responsible for what we become and, as we have seen, according to Kierkegaard there are no objective criteria for making decisions (truth is subjectivity). The individual must choose his or her own path, being formed as a person in the process.

Those who truly understand the situation we find ourselves in might very well experience *dread*, an emotion that needs to be distinguished from *fear*:

> ...fear is the recoil from threatening possibilities that lie outside a man's own conscious power, while dread is generated in him by the prodigious possibilities inherent in his own capacity to act.[1]

People will try to escape this feeling of dread, avoid making the crucial decision of how they will justify their lives. They may try just to live moment by moment, making only small, day to day decisions, attempting to avoid making long-term commitments to anything. But even our small decisions reveal a fundamental choice of an entire way of life; one chooses not just particular actions, but ways of living. If I decide to grade papers this afternoon and then decide to go to school early tomorrow morning to give extra help to a motivated student who is having difficulty with my course, rather than do some personal research or do something for my family, my choices show that I am making a commitment to teaching, to justifying my life as a person who will try to impart knowledge to, and guide, others.

There will be cynics who think it doesn't matter what choices we make; one's life will turn out badly, whatever one chooses:

> You listen to their exposition of the case and then say, "Yes, I perceive perfectly that there are two possibilities, one can either do this or that. My sincere opinion and my friendly counsel is as follows: Do it, or don't do it — you will regret both."[2]

---

[1] Stephen Crites, "Pseudonymous Authorship as Art and as Act," in Thompson, *Op. Cit.*, p. 187.
[2] *Either/Or, Op. Cit.*, p. 98.

Since "one knows very well that such is not the case," this is an entirely inappropriate response to the choices we face in life. It *does* matter — it matters very much — what we do.

Some people may try to avoid making the hard choice of how to justify their lives by doing what those around them expect them to do in whatever situations arise. They try to satisfy others' expectations rather than choose a path for themselves. Such people are merely a series of masks which they wear around others and, according to Kierkegaard, "in fact you are nothing; you are merely a relation to others."[1] At some point, though, it will be terribly important that you know who you are, what you stand for:

> Do you not know that there comes a midnight hour when everyone has to throw off his mask? Do you believe that life will always let itself be mocked? Do you think you can slip away a little before midnight in order to avoid this?[2]

There is a danger, in defining oneself through a series of masks one wears for others, that there will be nothing underneath when the "midnight hour" comes.[3]

Others may take too long in making the choice of a guiding principle for their lives and lose opportunities as a result. The twentieth century poet Sylvia Plath, in her semi-autobiographical novel *The Bell Jar*, depicted perhaps better than anyone ever has the tremendous responsibility put upon the person who fully appreciates the "either/or" options one has in life, how difficult it may be to choose, and how the options may vanish if one doesn't act in time, that "there comes at last an instant when there no longer is any question of an either/or, not because [one] has chosen but because [one] has neglected to choose"[4]:

> I saw my life branching out before me like the green fig tree in the story. From the tip of every branch. like a fat purple fig, a wonderful future beckoned and winked. One fig was a husband and a happy home and children, and another fig was a famous poet and another fig was a brilliant professor, and

---

[1] *Ibid.*, p. 99.

[2] *Ibid.*

[3] Compare with Nietzsche who claimed that "every profound spirit needs a mask." (*Beyond Good and Evil*, "The Free Spirit," Section 40)

[4] *Either/Or, Op. Cit.*, p. 103.

another fig was Ee Gee, the amazing editor, and another fig was Europe and Africa and South America, and another fig was Constantin and Socrates and Attila and a pack of other lovers with queer names and offbeat professions, and another fig was an Olympic lady crew champion, and beyond and above these figs were many more figs I couldn't quite make out.

I saw myself sitting in the crotch of this fig tree, starving to death, just because I couldn't make up my mind which of the figs I would choose. I wanted each and every one of them, but choosing one meant loosing all the rest, and, as I sat there, unable to decide, the figs began to wrinkle and go black, and, one by one, they plopped to the ground at my feet.[1]

So "it is important to choose and to choose in time."[2]

How do you choose between the different possible ways of justifying your life? According to Kierkegaard, it is important to test yourself. He would agree with Nietzsche who said:

> One has to test oneself...and do it at the right time. One should not dodge one's tests, though they may be the most dangerous game one could play and are tests that are taken in the end before no witness or judge but ourselves.[3]

You must put yourself, even if only imaginatively, in situations that force you to choose between actions which will reveal that you feel more strongly about one particular way of justifying your life than another. Kierkegaard helps us with this task by imaginatively creating/recreating pivotal dilemmas that force us to choose between entire ways of life. It's important that we try out different possibilities of ways of justifying our lives to see what is right for us.

How do we know if we've chosen rightly? As we've seen, there is no objective certainty. Instead, "in making a choice it is not so much a question of choosing the right as of the energy, the earnestness, the

---

[1] Sylvia Plath, *The Bell Jar*, Buccaneer Books, Cutchogue. N.Y., 1971, pp. 62-3.

[2] *Either/Or, Op. Cit.*, p. 104.

[3] *Beyond Good and Evil*, "The Free Spirit," Section 41 (translated by Walter Kaufmann).

pathos with which one chooses."¹ Although there is no objective criterion for the choice, subjectively there will be. We will feel that we are more suited to one of the options. Ideally, we will feel as if a path *has chosen us*, it will feel so right for us. When this happen, paradoxically,

> However astonishing it may seem,...compulsion can master [one] in such a way that there is no longer any question of choice — and then one chooses the right thing. At the hour of death most people choose the right thing.²

Three Spheres of Existence

> [N]ot one shall be forgotten who was great in the world. But each was great in his own way, and each in proportion to the greatness of that which he loved. For he who loved himself became great by himself, and he who loved other men became great by his selfless devotion, but he who loved God became greater than all.³

> My either/or does not in the first instance denote the choice between good and evil, it denotes the choice whereby one chooses good *and* evil/or excludes them.⁴

According to Kierkegaard, there are three basic options for giving coherence to one's life, for guiding principles to live by. He sometimes calls them "spheres of existence." Oversimplifying, as Kierkegaard does in the first quotation above, one has the choice of either living for *oneself* or living for *others* or living for *God*. He calls these three

---

¹ *Ibid.*, p. 106.
² *Journal*, 1850-54, *Op. Cit.*, p. 427.
³ *Fear and Trembling*, "A Panegyric Upon Abraham," in *Fear and Trembling and The Sickness Unto Death*, translated by Walter Lowrie, Princeton University Press, Princeton, N. J., 1974, p. 31.
⁴ *Either/Or*, *Op. Cit.*, p. 107.

spheres the **aesthetic**, the **ethical** and the **religious spheres** respectively.

Kierkegaard claims that these spheres are mutually exclusive and jointly exhaust the possibilities. In claiming that they are mutually exclusive, Kierkegaard would argue that although it is possible for a time to act in accordance with the guiding principle of two, or possibly even all three, of the spheres simultaneously, there will eventually come a time when one has to choose between them. Crisis situations will arise which force you to commit to one of them. This is why Kierkegaard recommends that you test yourself, if only imaginatively, to find out which one is right for you, preferably before a crisis situation arises. Kierkegaard's pseudonymous works give us imaginative tests to help us make the choice. "[E]ach work is in its own way designed to create a quiet crisis in the life of the reader that can be resolved only by his own decision."[1]

Do the three spheres of existence which Kierkegaard gives us jointly exhaust the possibilities? We must see how they are described to see if there are any other basic options for a guiding principle for one's life.

Before describing the three spheres, I must explain two somewhat controversial stances which I shall take with regard to Kierkegaard's depiction of them in his works. I believe that my stances are consistent with a plausible reading of Kierkegaard and that they will help to make Kierkegaard's overall philosophy more defensible. First, there are many passages (like the first one quoted above) in which Kierkegaard seems to telling us that the three spheres form a hierarchy, with the aesthetic sphere the lowest, then the ethical, and finally the religious sphere as the highest. It appears, in these passages, as though one should first leave the aesthetic way of thinking behind for the ethical and then, eventually, the ethical behind for the religious perspective.

We must remember, however, that Kierkegaard's famous pseudonymous works were written from particular limited perspectives and most of these were written from the perspective of someone who was convinced that the religious sphere was the highest so, of course, one can find passages like the first one given above which express this bias. Other works, which Kierkegaard signed his name to, reflect Kierkegaard's own *personal* choice of the religious sphere over the others; but this doesn't mean that this sphere will be right for everyone. We must balance these passages which "pitch" the religious sphere

---

[1] Crites, *Op. Cit.*, p. 224.

against Kierkegaard's central idea that there is no objective truth which we must all accept as to how we should live our lives. I believe that Kierkegaard thinks that all three spheres are viable options for guiding principles for a person's life. He spends more time depicting the religious sphere in a favorable light because it was his own personal choice and because his depiction of it, as we shall see, is entirely new and highly controversial. The two other spheres have had defenders over the years, but not the religious sphere as Kierkegaard understands it.

The second stance I will take is to broaden the typical depiction of the aesthetic sphere. Instead of focusing entirely on Volume I of *Either/Or*, the only work of Kierkegaard's written from an aesthetic sphere bias, I shall put more weight on the first quotation I've given above from *Fear and Trembling* which gives a more general view of the aesthetic sphere. I think that there are options within each of the three spheres, some higher and lower, and to focus on one way one can live an aesthetic, ethical or religious life to the exclusion of all others would misrepresent the three basic options we have as to how we can justify our lives and unfairly weaken the argument that the three spheres of existence are all genuine options and jointly exhaust the possibilities.

The first option for a guiding principle for one's life, on a broad understanding of the **aesthetic sphere**, is "to live for oneself." Kierkegaard intends the aesthetic sphere to cover a general perspective which may be realized in a number of different lifestyles. Living for oneself may take a very primitive form of living to satisfy immediate personal desires, leading to a life which moves from one debauch to another. An example would be the life of Don Juan. A life like Don Juan's is probably a self-defeating way of life, Kierkegaard points out, because the repetition of similar pleasures causes boredom and we are probably not psychologically constituted to be able to live a nonstop life of pleasure.

A higher level of aesthetic life is represented by the artist, in the broadest sense of the term "artist," who lives for self-fulfillment, that is to develop his or her talents and abilities to the fullest. One can think of the lives of Mozart or Wagner, and a number of great painters and writers, as exemplifying this philosophy of life. In general, the person living within the aesthetic sphere is concerned with personal satisfaction. Nietzsche's overman would, presumably, be the heroic ideal for this sphere of existence. Nietzsche said of his overman:

...his word pronounced *selfishness* blessed, the wholesome, healthy selfishness that wells from a powerful soul — from a powerful soul to which belongs the high body, beautiful, triumphant, refreshing, around which everything becomes a mirror — the subtle persuasive body, the dancer whose parable and epitome is the self-enjoying soul.[1]

The **ethical sphere** is one in which the individual thinks in terms of what's best for the community, ideally *all*, not just for himself or herself. An ethical life requires the individual to take others into account and perform those actions which would be best for all concerned. One thinks in terms of universals, absolutes, good and evil, rather than just what pleases or displeases oneself. The individual is subservient to the universal.

There are many ethical theories which attempt to spell out what is good and evil and so there are many ways in which one could try to live an ethical life. The theory which Kierkegaard was particularly aware of and which, at the time, was considered to be the epitome of the ethical way of thinking was Kant's Categorical Imperative: *Act always in such a way that one could wish the maxim (or principle) of one's action could become universal law.* For Kant, this was the only rational way to behave. One should not make an exception of oneself; what is right for one person to do should be right for anyone else in similar circumstances. Kant's secondary imperative, a corollary to the Categorical Imperative — *never treat others as a mean's to one's own ends, but always as ends in themselves* — further emphasized the idea that one should not think only of oneself when deciding how to act.

Since Kant's, and Kierkegaard's, day other ethical theories have been proposed — Utilitarianism in various forms, Ross's theory of prima facie duties, virtue-based ethics, Rawls' social contract theory, etc. — which are all examples of ways to live one's life within the ethical sphere. There are certainly many options for particular guiding principles which all fall under the general heading of trying to do what is best for all, rather than just oneself.

In *Either/Or*, Kierkegaard considers an example of a test of whether one is willing to live an ethical rather than aesthetic life: contemplating getting married. To understand properly what getting married entails, you should see that you must leave behind thinking

---

[1] *Thus Spoke Zarathustra*, "On the Three Evils," Section 2 (translated by Walter Kaufmann)

only about yourself. Marriage involves creating a community of two people — and possibly others, if children follow — and each must now think about what is best for that community whenever decisions must be made. According to Kierkegaard, then, the decision to get married involves — or at any rate *should* involve — choosing the ethical way of life over the aesthetic.

The third sphere of existence, the final option for a guiding principle for one's life, is the **religious sphere**: One can live for God. Most people are shocked to learn that Kierkegaard considers the religious sphere to be distinct from the ethical sphere. Surely one shouldn't have to choose between the ethical and the religious? Kierkegaard thinks that we do have to choose between them because his understanding of the religious sphere, derived from his study of Christian texts, is that: (1) it is irrational, (2) a religious believer oversteps the universal is establishing a one-to-one relationship with God, and (3) the believer may be asked by God to do something unethical as a test of faith. None of these characteristics of religious sphere can be reconciled with the ethical way of thinking. The ethical is rational, the ethical individual must be subservient to the universal, and there are no exceptions to doing what is ethically right. To do what is ethically wrong is to sin, period.

First and foremost, Kierkegaard characterizes the religious sphere, in contrast to earlier philosophers and theologians, as essentially *irrational*. One believes in God, one has faith, in spite of — and actually because of — the absurdity or paradoxicalness of the belief. According to Christianity, for instance, God, an eternal and infinite being, was one with Christ, a temporal and finite being. And one should expect, if one is a believer, that with God *all* things are possible, even things which are physically and logically impossible. Of course this is irrational, but according to Kierkegaard, that is the nature of religious faith.

Furthermore, the believer, in standing "in an absolute relation to the absolute," is "higher than the universal" which could only be considered to be a temptation, and therefore wrong, from the ethical perspective:

> The ethical as such is the universal, and as the universal it applies to everyone....the particular individual is the individual who has his *telos* in the universal, and his ethical task is to express himself constantly in it, to abolish his particularity in

order to become the universal. As soon as the individual would assert himself in his particularity over against the universal he sins....

...faith is this paradox, that the particular is higher than the universal....[1]

Finally, according to Kierkegaard, to live within the religious sphere, one must put God before all others; just as to live within the ethical sphere, one must put the welfare of all ahead of one's own personal welfare. One has an absolute duty toward God in the religious sphere. Kierkegaard takes passages like the story of Abraham and Isaac and the following one from Luke, in the Bible, very seriously:

In Luke 14:26, as everybody knows, there is a striking doctrine about the absolute duty toward God: "If any man cometh unto me and hateth not his own father and mother and wife and children and brethern and sisters, yea, and his own life also, he cannot be my disciple." This is a hard saying, who can bear to hear it? ....

One can easily perceive that if there is to be any sense in this passage, it must be understood literally. God it is who requires absolute love.[2]

Why would one want to believe in God, if it is irrational and could conflict with the ethical way of life? Because one feels the need of God in one's life; one is not entirely happy in this earthly life. In *The Sickness Unto Death*, Kierkegaard argues that, from the perspective of the religious sphere, anyone who does not have a relationship with God is, to some degree or other, in despair because he or she has not recognized or accepted the eternal part of himself or herself.

Just as there are higher and lower examples of living within the aesthetic sphere, there is a higher and lower type of religious individual. The heroic ideal of a person living within the religious sphere is the "knight of faith" and a lesser type of religious believer is the "knight of infinite resignation." I shall have more to say about each type of individual in the next section on Faith.

There is an interesting similarity between the aesthetic and the religious spheres. In both of these spheres, individuals assert

---

[1] *Fear and Trembling*, in Lowrie, *Op. Cit.*, pp. 64-5.
[2] *Ibid.*, pp. 82-3.

themselves in their particularity against the universal. But there is an important difference, to be discussed at greater length in the next section. Whereas aesthetic individuals *want* to assert themselves in their particularity, for religious believers, asserting themselves in their particularity "is not an immediate instinct of the heart." These individuals would love to do the ethically correct action, would love to act in accordance with the universal, but cannot due to their absolute duty to God:

> He who believes that it is easy enough to be the individual can always be sure that he is not a knight of faith, for vagabonds and roving geniuses are not men of faith. The knight of faith knows, on the other hand, that it is glorious to belong to the universal....he knows that it is terrible to be born outside the universal....[1]

The ethical sphere is certainly the most favored sphere, the one the majority of people prefer. This is understandable since the ethical way of thinking best protects the majority's interests. If one is attracted to either of the other spheres, one will certainly have to consider very carefully the choice between this other sphere — either the aesthetic or the religious sphere — and the ethical sphere. This is why Kierkegaard says that the important either/or choice in life is not "the choice between good and evil," which both belong within the ethical sphere, but "the choice whereby one chooses good *and* evil/or excludes them."

Now we are ready to consider the question of whether there are any other options for basic guiding principles for one's life than living for oneself, for others or for God. What other options could there be, particularly if you consider living for God as, in a general way, choosing to live for a being(s) greater than the finite beings whose existence we perceive? Either one believes in a greater being(s) or one doesn't. If one believes in the existence of a greater being(s), one can live for that being/those beings. Within the realm of finite beings, we have the basic choice of focusing on ourselves or taking other beings into account (and various theories about how best to do that). There don't seem to be any other basic options, although there certainly are many ways to live one's life which can fall under these three basic options.

---

[1] *Fear and Trembling*, in Lowrie, *Op. Cit.*, p. 86.

We can ask, however, whether we must have a guiding principle *at all* to live our lives by.[1] It is certainly possible to be a member of the human race without being either an aesthetic, ethical or religious person. One could refuse to live a reflective, principled life. If so, one would be a very poor specimen of a human being, according to Kierkegaard. Since the three spheres "are modes of existing in and by which a free being like man constitutes his own selfhood,"[2] as we shall see in a later section, such an individual isn't properly a self, even though he or she may be a biological human being. In any case, the existence of individuals who live unprincipled lives does not give us an alternative *principled* way of life.

Can we change the guiding principle of our lives? Certainly we can and do. Sometimes we move from one sphere to another, from, say, the aesthetic to the ethical, or the ethical to the religious spheres. But it is also possible to make a more subtle change from one ethical principle to another, or from a lower to higher form of aesthetic or religious existence, and remain within the same basic sphere of existence. A man who tires of living for one sexual conquest after another may decide to get married, leaving the aesthetic for the ethical sphere, or concentrate instead on the development of his musical talent, moving from a lower to a higher level of aesthetic existence.

On what basis do we choose one of these spheres initially, or change from one sphere to another? Remembering that "truth is subjectivity" according to Kierkegaard, the reasons for doing so "are not logical but *psychological*; they are not logically compelling, but they may be compelling for some individual."[3] A radically free choice is involved which amounts to choosing to be a particular type of self, or changing one's self, and also adopting a particular view of, or changing one's view of, the world.

Faith

The realm of faith is...not a class for numskulls in the sphere of the intellectual, or an asylum for the feeble-minded. Faith constitutes a sphere all by itself, and every

---

[1] See Crites, *Op. Cit.*, pp. 184-5.

[2] Mackey, *Op. Cit.*, p. 276.

[3] Solomon, *Op. Cit.*, p. 96.

misunderstanding of Christianity may at once be recognized by its transforming it into a doctrine, transferring it to the sphere of the intellectual.[1]

The highest form of existence within the religious sphere — the type of individual who is considered to be the hero within this sphere — is the **knight of faith**. To appreciate what it means to be a knight of faith, we must understand what Kierkegaard means by faith and how a knight of faith is different from both the **tragic (ethical) hero** and the type of individual who is at a lower level within the religious sphere, the **knight of infinite resignation**.

Kierkegaard says that "without risk there is no faith." If we *know* that God exists, if we have proof of His existence, there would be no need of, or place for, faith. Since we don't have proof of God's existence, the possibility of faith exists.

What is also necessary for faith, besides objective uncertainty, is a passionate commitment on the part of the individual to believe in God despite this uncertainty:

> Faith is precisely the contradiction between the infinite passion of the individual's inwardness and the objective uncertainty. If I am capable of grasping God objectively, I do not believe, but precisely because I cannot do this I must believe.[2]

Furthermore, according to Kierkegaard, the greater the uncertainty — the greater the risk the believer takes in believing — the greater the faith. The maximum that one could have in terms of uncertainty is to believe in something which is logically impossible, something contradictory. This is precisely the situation that Christians, and perhaps other religious believers as well, find themselves in. Christianity rests on a paradox, on that which is literally absurd:

> What now is the absurd? The absurd is — that the eternal truth has come into being in time, that God has come into being, has been born, has grown up, and so forth, has come

---

[1] *Concluding Unscientific Postscript*, in Bretall, *Op. Cit.*, p. 231.
[2] "The Subjective Truth: Inwardness, Truth is Subjectivity," *Concluding Unscientific Postscript, Op. Cit.*, p. 215.

into being precisely like any other individual human being, quite indistinguishable from any other individuals.[1]

> Christianity...has proclaimed itself as the *Paradox*...and an absurdity to the understanding. It is impossible to express more strongly the fact that...objectivity merely repels...[2]

Since to believe in God amounts to making a personal commitment to something which is intellectually absurd, the greatest passion or "inwardness" must exist to compensate for there not being any possible objective security, and this is true faith as Kierkegaard understands it:

> ...the greater the risk, the greater the faith; the more objective security, the less inwardness...and the less objective security, the more profound the possible inwardness. When the paradox is paradoxical in itself, it repels the individual by virtue of its absurdity, and the corresponding passion of inwardness is faith.[3]

There is nothing intellectual about Christianity, according to Kierkegaard, because that would destroy faith. Faith requires passion and "passion and reflection are generally exclusive of one another."[4] Christianity is not to be thought of as a doctrine. If Christianity were to be thought of primarily as a doctrine, not only would it become intellectual, which is antithetical to faith, but God would no longer be the focus of attention:

> The object of faith is the reality of another, and the relationship is one of infinite interest. The object of faith is not a doctrine, for then the relationship would be intellectual, and it would be of importance not to botch it, but to realize the maximum intellectual relationship. The object of faith is not a teacher with a doctrine; for when a teacher has a doctrine, the

---

[1] *Ibid.*, p. 220.

[2] *Ibid.*, p. 222.

[3] *Ibid.*, p. 219.

[4] *Ibid.*, "Conclusion: What it is to Become a Christian," *Concluding Unscientific Postscript, Op. Cit.*, p. 255.

doctrine is *eo ipso* more important than the teacher....The
object of faith is the reality of the teacher, that the teacher
really exists...."Do you or do you not suppose that he has
really existed?"[1]

To sum up, faith according to Kierkegaard, is a personal decision
to believe in the existence of God —"faith...implies an act of the will"[2]
— despite the fact that it is absurd that God should exist, and the
decision to believe is made with infinite passion:

> *Faith is the objective uncertainty along with the repulsion of*
> *the absurd held in the passion of inwardness, which is*
> *inwardness potentiated to the highest degree.* This formula fits
> only the believer, no one else, not a lover, not an enthusiast,
> not a thinker, but simply and solely the believer who is related
> to the absolute paradox.[3]

In *Fear and Trembling*, Kierkegaard gives us an example of a true
believer, a knight of faith: Abraham. This book — a pseudonymous
work written from the perspective of one who stands in awe of
Abraham's faith, but cannot emulate it — recounts the story of
Abraham and Isaac and deduces certain lessons about faith from it.
In Genesis, Chapter 22, we find the crucial passage:

> *And God tempted Abraham and said unto him, Take*
> *Isaac, thine only son, whom thou lovest, and get thee into the*
> *land of Moriah, and offer him there for a burnt offering upon*
> *the mountain which I will show thee.*

Kierkegaard reminds us that Abraham was "God's elect, in whom
the Lord was well pleased" and that he had already been tested:

> By faith Abraham received the promise that in his seed all
> the races of the world would be blessed. Time passed, the
> possibility was there, Abraham believed; time passed, it

---

[1] "The Subjective Thinker," *Concluding Unscientific Postscript, Op.
Cit.*, p. 230.
[2] *Journal*, 1834.
[3] "Conclusion: What it Means to Become a Christian," *Concluding
Unscientific Postscript, Op. Cit.*, p. 255.

became unreasonable, Abraham believed....Abraham became old, Sarah became a laughingstock in the land....

Then there was joy in Abraham's house, when Sarah became a bride on the day of their golden wedding.[1]

After waiting fifty years for Isaac, after fighting with Time and preserving his faith, now Abraham was asked to do the unthinkable:

> So all was lost, more dreadfully than if it had never come to pass! So the Lord was only making sport of Abraham! He made miraculously the preposterous actual, and now in turn He would annihilate it.[2]

Kierkegaard has us imagine what it must have been like for Abraham to embrace Sarah, who in turn kissed Isaac — her pride and joy — good-bye, and start out on the journey to Mount Moriah. He could not tell Sarah the purpose of the journey; she would not understand. How could *anyone* understand? For three days Abraham and Isaac journeyed to Mount Moriah in silence. There was no getting the ordeal over quickly. What went through Abraham's mind? Try to imagine an old man, who had spent his whole life waiting for the son God had promised him, and whom he loved more than life itself, now about to kill this son because God required it of him as one more test of his faith. "Is there no compassion for the venerable oldling, none for the innocent child?"[3]

On the fourth day, they reached the mountain and Abraham prepared to sacrifice his son, who must have been terrified when he at last realized the purpose of the journey. Kierkegaard tells us that Abraham:

> ...did not doubt, he did not look anxiously to the right or to the left, he did not challenge heaven with his prayers. He knew that it was God the Almighty who was trying him, he knew that it was the hardest sacrifice that could be required of him; but he knew also that no sacrifice was too hard when God required it — and he drew the knife.
>
> Who gave strength to Abraham's arm? Who held his right

---

[1] *Fear and Trembling, Op. Cit.*, pp. 32-3.

[2] *Ibid.*, pp. 33-4.

[3] *Ibid.*, p. 34.

hand up so that it did no fall limp at his side? He who gazes at this becomes paralyzed. Who gave strength to Abraham's soul, so that his eyes did not grow dim, so that he saw neither Isaac nor the ram? He who gazes at this becomes blind.[1]

At the mention of the ram, we remember that in the end Abraham did not have to sacrifice Isaac, that the ram was substituted instead. Does this make it all right then, and somehow make Abraham's ordeal less harrowing? According to Kierkegaard, "people are curious about the result... — they want to know nothing about dread, distress, the paradox."[2] What people don't want to dwell on is the fact that Abraham must have been fully prepared to sacrifice Isaac or the ram wouldn't have been waiting; he wouldn't have passed the test "How many were made sleepless" by the story, as they should have been, Kierkegaard asks.

Instead of letting the full weight — the *terrible* weight — sink in that Abraham was prepared to kill his own son, people instead try to sum up the story of Abraham and Isaac in general terms: "The great thing was that he loved God so much that he was willing to sacrifice to Him the best." But, as Kierkegaard points out, "the best" is very vague. If people think in terms of, say, money and imagine giving away one's fortune to help the poor if God asks it and believe that Abraham's sacrifice is similar:

> What they leave out of Abraham's history is dread; for to money I have no ethical obligation, but to the son the father has the highest and most sacred obligation.[3]

What people don't want to think about is the fact that Abraham was asked, by God, to do something *unethical* as a test of faith. From the perspective of the ethical sphere, one would say that Abraham was about to murder Isaac. Could there be anything more wrong, from the ethical perspective, than that a parent — who brought a child into the world and has therefore has the most solemn obligation to protect the child — would turn around and take the life of that child? The tension between the ethical and religious perspectives must be recognized and not glossed over:

---

[1] *Ibid.*, p. 36.

[2] *Ibid.*, p. 74.

[3] *Ibid.*, p. 39.

The ethical expression for what Abraham did is, that he would murder Isaac; the religious expression is, that he would sacrifice Isaac; but precisely in this contradiction consists the dread which can well make a man sleepless, and yet Abraham is not what he is without this dread.[1]

To fully comprehend the dread that is a part of the story of Abraham and Isaac, Kierkegaard has us compare Abraham's, a knight of faith's, situation with the situation of a **tragic (ethical) hero**. The tragic hero is the highest being, what one can aspire to be if the occasion calls for it, *within the ethical sphere*. Recall, for example, the story of King Agamemnon. During the Trojan War, King Agamemnon was forced to sacrifice his beloved daughter Iphigenia for the welfare of his country. He was able to rise to the occasion of putting a higher ethical duty to his people ahead of the lower personal duty to his child. Agamemnon's and Abraham's circumstances may appear similar — each was prepared to sacrifice a beloved child — yet Agamemnon remained within the ethical sphere, while Abraham was prepared to overstep the ethical entirely.

Agamemnon's action could be understood and admired by others:

> ...the king...must act royally. And though solitary pain forces its way into his breast,...soon the whole nation [was] cognizant of his pain, but also cognizant of his exploit, that for the welfare of the whole he was willing to sacrifice her, his daughter, the lovely young maiden.[2]

There was no way, on the other hand, that others could understand and applaud what Abraham was about to do. There was no higher ethical purpose for his action. Thus:

> The difference between the tragic hero and Abraham is clearly evident. The tragic hero still remains within the ethical. He lets one expression of the ethical find its *telos* in a higher expression of the ethical....
> With Abraham the situation was different. By his act he

---

[1] *Ibid.*, p. 41.

[2] *Ibid.*, p. 68.

overstepped the ethical entirely and possessed a higher *telos* outside of it....[1]

Another difference between the tragic hero and the knight of faith is that whereas the tragic hero expects to lose something in performing the heroic action, the knight of faith doesn't. Agamemnon expects to lose Iphigenia, but Abraham doesn't expect to lose Isaac, at least not in the long run:

> ...even at the instant when the knife glittered he believed...that God would not require Isaac.[2]

Suppose the ram had not been there and he did have to kill Isaac:

> Let us go further. We let Isaac be really sacrificed. Abraham believed. He did not believe that some day he would be blessed in the beyond, but that he would be happy here in the world. God could give him a new Isaac, could recall to life him who had been sacrificed. He believed by virtue of the absurd; for all human reckoning had long since ceased to function.[3]

Of course this is irrational; but that, as we have seen, is the nature of religious faith. This brings up the difference between the knight of faith and the **knight of infinite resignation**, an individual within the religious sphere who is at the last stage prior to faith. Unlike the knight of faith, the knight of infinite resignation "cannot shut [his] eyes and plunge confidently into the absurd."

The knight of infinite resignation, recognizing the eternal part of himself which is not at home in this life, gives himself up into the hands of God. With a great leap he "pass[es] into infinity" and he renounces all claim to the finite:

> With infinte resignation he has drained the cup of life's profound sadness, he knows the bliss of the infinite, he

---

[1] *Ibid.*, p. 69.

[2] *Ibid.*, p. 46.

[3] *Ibid.*, pp. 46-7.

[experiences] the pain of renouncing everything, the dearest things he possesses in the world....[1]

The pseudonymous author of *Fear and Trembling*, who is merely a knight of infinite resignation, imagines what he would do in Abraham's situation:

> I know very well what I would have done. I would not have been cowardly enough to stay at home, neither would I have laid down or sauntered along the way, nor have forgotten the knife, so that there might be a little delay — I am pretty well convinced that I would have been there on the stroke of the clock and would have had everything in order, perhaps I would have arrived too early in order to get through with it sooner. But I also know what else I would have done. The very instant I mounted the horse I would have said to myself, "Now all is lost. God requires Isaac, I sacrifice him, and with him my joy — yet God is love and continues to be that for me;....What Abraham found easiest, I would have found hard, namely to be joyful again with Isaac; for he who with all the infinity of his soul...has performed the infinite movement [of resignation] and cannot do more, only retains Isaac with pain.[2]

The knight of faith, on the other hand, first makes the movement of infinite resignation, but then — because of his faith which allows him to believe that with God all things are possible — he is able to get the finite back, and it's just as wonderful to him as if he'd never given it up in the first place. This second movement, which involves giving up one's reason, is what most people cannot do; but it shows, according to Kierkegaard, that they do not truly have faith. Even though it is extremely difficult to have faith —"when I...think of Abraham...I am paralyzed" — it is clear that for Kierkegaard it is the most wonderful thing:

> ...to be able to lose one's reason, and therefore the whole of finiteness of which reason is the broker, and then by virtue of the absurd to gain precisely the same finiteness — that appalls

---

[1] *Ibid.*, p. 51.
[2] *Ibid.*, pp. 45-6.

my soul, but I do not for this cause say that it is something lowly, since on the contrary it is the only prodigy.[1]

Because the knight of faith expects to have his finite desires satisfied, he can appear to others to be an individual who is leading an *aesthetic* life. His "outward appearance bears a striking resemblance...to Philistinism."

> He takes delight in everything, and whenever one sees him taking part in a particular pleasure, he does it with the persistence which is the mark of the earthly man whose soul is absorbed in such things....On his way [home from work] he reflects that his wife has surely a special little warm dish prepared for him....If he were to meet a man like-minded, he could continue as far as East Gate to discourse with him about that dish, with a passion befitting a hotel chef. As it happens, he hasn't four pence to his name, and yet he fully and firmly believes that his wife has that dainty dish for him.[2]

Despite the fact that his *outward* appearance is that of a very ordinary person who enjoys life —"Good Lord, is this the man? Is it really he? Why, he looks like a tax-collector!" is how Kierkegaard describes what he might look like — *inside* there is a man who has made two movements which are beyond what the aesthetic individual would be capable of making. He has, first, given up his claims on the finite by making the movement of infinite resignation. Then — and this is what makes him a knight of faith — he confidently plunges into the Absurd and gets the finite back: "He resigned everything infinitely, and then he grasped everything again by virtue of the absurd."[3] It follows from this that "faith, therefore, is not an aesthetic emotion;" "it is not an immediate instinct of the heart" because "it has resignation as its presupposition."

One cannot go directly into the stage of having faith, according to Kierkegaard, but only through infinite resignation:

> The infinite resignation is the last stage prior to faith, so that one who has not made this movement has not faith; for

---

[1] *Ibid.*, p. 47.
[2] *Ibid.*, p. 50.
[3] *Ibid.*, p. 51.

only in the infinite resignation do I become clear to myself with respect to my eternal validity, and only then can there be any question of grasping existence by faith.[1]

Kierkegaard wrote *Fear and Trembling* for Regine. The motto that he chose for the title page, a quotation from Hamman —"What Tarquinius Superbus spoke in his garden with the poppies was understood by his son, but not by the messenger"[2] — indicated that Regine would understand the book, even if no one else did. Just as Abraham was called upon to sacrifice Isaac, whom he loved more than anything in the world, because God required it, so Kierkegaard had believed that he must give up Regine, the great love of his life, to serve God.

At one point in *Fear and Trembling*, Kierkegaard makes it even more obvious that he is really writing about his relationship to Regine:

> A young swain falls in love with a princess, and the whole content of his life consists in this love, and yet the situation is such that it is impossible for it to be realized....by infinite resignation he is reconciled with existence. Love for that princess became for him the expression for an eternal love, assumed a religious character, was transfigured into a love for the Eternal Being, which did to be sure deny him the fulfillment of his love, yet reconciled him again by the eternal consciousness of its validity in the form of eternity, which no reality can take from him.[3]

Kierkegaard realized, by the time that he wrote this book that he was only a knight of infinite resignation. He wrote in his journal: "If I had had faith, I would have remained with Regine." He imagines a knight of faith "in the role just described:"

---

[1] *Ibid.*, p. 57.

[2] Tarquinius did not trust the messenger who had come from his son, asking him what he should do with the people of Gabbii, so he took the messenger into the garden and had him watch while he cut off the heads of the tallest poppies. He knew that his son would understand by this that he should bring about the death of the most prominent men in the city.

[3] *Ibid.*, pp. 52-4.

He makes exactly the same movements as the other knight, infinitely renounces his claim to the love which is the content of his life, he is reconciled in pain; but then occurs the prodigy, he makes still another movement more wonderful than all, for he says, "I believe nevertheless that I shall get her, in virtue, that is, of the absurd, in virtue of the fact that with God all things are possible."[1]

Kierkegaard did not himself have the faith which he so admired in Abraham, but he thought "it must be glorious to get the princess...." He maintains that it is extremely rare to have faith, and yet "no [person] is excluded from it." All that is required is *passion*, of which we all are capable: "that in which all human life is unified is passion, and faith is a passion."[2]

What concerns most readers about Kierkegaard's depiction of the religious sphere, which he derives from passages like the story of Abraham and Isaac, is that one may be asked by God to do something unethical as a test of faith. This gives rise to the paradox that, from the religious perspective, the individual, in his relationship to God, is higher than the universal; whereas, from the ethical perspective, the individual who believes he can act in opposition to the universal is in temptation, he would sin. How can one distinguish between an Abraham, a knight of faith, and a Charles Manson or Reverend Jim Jones, who thought they were called by God to kill human beings? Kierkegaard has something to say about this problem:

> That for the particular individual this paradox may easily be mistaken for a temptation is indeed true, but one ought not for this reason to conceal it. That the whole constitution of many persons may be such that this paradox repels them is indeed true, but one ought not for this reason to make something different in order to be able to possess it, but...those who possess faith should take care to set up certain criteria so that one might distinguish the paradox from a temptation.

What "criteria" could be set up to distinguish a murderer from an Abraham? "How then does the individual assure himself that he is

---

[1] *Ibid.*, p. 57.
[2] *Ibid.*, p. 77.

justified?" The main test Kierkegaard gives is a subjective one: *The individual must not want to do the killing.*

> ...when God requires Isaac he must love him if possible even more dearly,...it is this love for Isaac which...makes his act a sacrifice.[1]

We can say that "if he does not love like Abraham, then every thought of offering Isaac would be not a trial but a base temptation."[2] The knight of faith wants to do the ethically correct action — this is what tempts him — whereas the murderer doesn't want to do the ethically correct action:

> What ordinarily tempts a man is that which would keep him from doing his duty, but in this case [the case of the knight of faith] the temptation is itself the ethical...which would keep him from doing God's will.[3]

It will impossible for one person to judge whether another individual is sinning or undergoing a test of faith: "Whether the individual is in temptation or is a knight of faith only the individual can decide."[4] Part of the problem for determining whether another individual is being tested by God lies in the fact that the knight of faith "absolutely cannot make himself intelligible to anybody," not even to another knight of faith:

> The one knight of faith can render no aid to the other. Either the individual becomes a knight of faith by assuming the burden of the paradox, or he never becomes one. In these regions partnership is unthinkable....only the individual becomes a knight of faith as the particular individual, and this is the greatness of this knighthood...but this is also its terror....[5]

---

[1] *Ibid.*, p. 84.
[2] *Ibid.*, p. 42.
[3] *Ibid.*, p. 70.
[4] *Ibid.*, p. 89.
[5] *Ibid.*, p. 82.

The terror lies in the silence, in not being able to be understood by any other human being. Unlike the ethical hero whose actions can be understood —"all he does is in the light of the revealed" — the knight of faith when tested appears to be all too similar to the demoniac: "I stumble upon the paradox, either the divine or the demoniac, for silence is both."[1] The knight of faith walks

> ...a solitary path, narrow and steep; he knows that it is terrible to be born outside the universal, to walk without meeting a single traveler.[2]

"Purity of Heart"

> ...the thing is not to have many thoughts, but to hold fast to *one* thought. (*Journal*, 1841)

In *Fear and Trembling* Kierkegaard tells us that to make the first movement towards faith, one must have "purity of heart"; one must be able to put all one's energy towards a single thing, put all one's eggs into a single basket. This is what is required to be a knight of infinite resignation, the first step towards faith:

> ...for the first thing, the knight will have the power to concentrate the whole content of life and the whole significance of reality in one single wish. If a man lacks this concentration, this intensity, if his soul from the beginning is dispersed in the multifarious, he never comes to the point of making the movement, he will deal shrewdly in life like the capitalists who invest their money in all sorts of securities, so as to gain on the one what they lose on the other....[3]

Most people want to hedge their bets, rather than put all their eggs into one basket. There is more security in that approach, less of a likelihood of disappointment; but the rewards are much less as well. To

---

[1] *Ibid.*, p. 97.

[2] *Ibid.*, p. 86.

[3] *Ibid.*, p. 53.

achieve greatness in any field one must throw oneself completely in a single direction, whatever one chooses. This is what Kierkegaard means by having "purity of heart."

In *Purity of Heart*, one of the *Edifying Discourses in Various Spirits* published in 1847 under his own name, Kierkegaard develops this idea still further. He takes the phrase "purity of heart" from the Apostle James' words in his Epistle, Chapter 4, verse 8:

> *Draw nigh to God and he will draw nigh to you. Cleanse your hands, ye sinners; and purify your hearts, ye double-minded.*

Kierkegaard argues, in this work, that those who do not have purity of heart, those who are unable to will one thing are, whether they recognize it or not, in despair because they are pulled in different directions. For "what is it to despair other than to have two wills!" There is no unity to their lives. They are torn apart by conflicting impulses. Those who are divided in this way will take refuge in "busyness," scurrying from one task to another, anything to avoid facing their despair over not having found the one thing they are prepared to live and die for, or being afraid of making a real commitment to anything.

Kierkegaard also argues that many things people live for are incompatible with having purity of heart because they are not single things, even though they might appear to be so: "pleasure and honor and riches and power and all that this world has to offer only appear to be one thing."[1] Consider pleasure, for example. Variety is crucial for the lover of pleasure.

> Is variety, then, to will one thing that shall ever remain the same? On the contrary, it is to will one thing that must never be the same. It is to will a multitude of things. And a person who wills in this fashion is not only double-minded but is at odds with himself. For such a man wills first one thing and then immediately wills the opposite, because the oneness of pleasure is a snare and a delusion....something new! It was change he cried out for....[2]

---

[1] *Purity of Heart*, in Bretall, *Op. Cit.*, p. 273.

[2] *Ibid.*, pp. 273-4.

Pleasure, then, is not one thing. What is pleasurable at one moment can change into the very opposite at the next moment. "Carried to its extreme limit, what is pleasure other then disgust?"

It is similarly the case with honor, riches and power, none of which are static. Honor, riches and power depend on other people who may disagree with each other as to who should receive them, and so the seeker of these "goods" is also pulled in different directions. Kierkegaard, further, points out that to attain these things people "must grovel," be agreeable to those they dislike, even betray those they most respect: "to attain honor [and other worldly goods] means to despise oneself after one has attained the pinnacle of honor."

Therefore to have purity of heart, one must seek something which is unified. "To will one thing cannot," according to Kierkegaard, "mean to will what is not one thing, but only seems to be so." It must also be unchangeable. It cannot depend on public opinion. It must be some single constant thing which one can go on willing, even as other things change:

> Shall a man in truth will one thing, then this one thing that he wills must be such that it remains unaltered in all changes, so that by willing it he can win immutability. If it changes continually, then he himself becomes changeable, double-minded, and unstable. And this continual change is nothing else than impurity.[1]

An obvious candidate for a thing which does not change, in Kierkegaard's eyes, is the Good, something to which we are all attracted. Much as Socrates had argued, Kierkegaard maintains that people cannot consistently and for any length of time desire anything which conflicts with the Good. At some point they will feel "an agonizing longing for the Good" and then they will see that they have "two wills" and so lack purity of heart.

Kierkegaard believed that he himself had purity of heart. In the autobiographical work *The Point of View for My Work as an Author*, written in 1848, he gave this assessment of his own life:

> It was the cause of Christianity he served, his life from childhood on being marvelously fitted for such a service. Thus he carried to completion the work of reflection, the task of

---

[1] *Ibid.*, p. 276.

translating completely into terms of reflection, what it means to become a Christian. His purity of heart was to will only one thing. What his contemporaries complained of during his lifetime, that he would not abate the price, would not give in — this very thing is the eulogy pronounced upon him by after ages....[1]

What Kierkegaard would wish for us all is that we would each find, as he did, that single thing for which we can live and die. Having "purity of heart" gives a direction to one's life, a sense of purpose, a cure from the stress caused by conflicting desires.

Passion

> ...he who is lost through passion has not lost as much as he who [has] lost passion.... (*Concluding Unscientific Postscript*)

To make a commitment to a single thing, *passion* is needed. Unfortunately, Kierkegaard thought it was characteristic of his own age for people to be lacking in passion, and I suspect that it's rare in any age for people to have what Kierkegaard means by passion.

It's important, first, to know that Kierkegaard contrasts passion with reflection and objectivity:

> The psychologist generally regards it as a sure sign that a man is beginning to give up passion when he wishes to treat the object of it objectively. Passion and reflection are generally exclusive of one another.[2]

Furthermore, according to Kierkegaard, it is a negative thing to lose passion in favor of reflection or objectivity: "Becoming objective in this way is always retrogression."

Second, the strong emotion Kierkegaard calls passion may lead to unethical behavior. But Kierkegaard is less concerned with this possibility than that people are not passionate:

---

[1] *The Point of View for my Work as an Author*, in Bretall, *Op. Cit.*, p. 339.
[2] *Concluding Unscientific Postscript*, in Bretall, *Op. Cit.*, p. 255.

> Let others complain that the age is wicked; my complaint is
> that it is wretched, for it lacks passion. Men's thoughts are
> thin and flimsy like lace...The thoughts of their hearts are too
> paltry to be sinful....Their lusts are dull and sluggish, their
> passions sleepy. They do their duty....This is the reason my
> soul always turns back to the Old Testament and to
> Shakespeare. I feel those who speak there are at least human
> beings: they hate, they love, they murder their enemies, and
> curse their descendants throughout all generations, they sin.[1]

This passage was written from the perspective of an advocate of the
aesthetic way of life, and Kierkegaard certainly isn't recommending a
life of sin; but it seems clear that he is less concerned about the
possibility of our sinning than that we don't throw ourselves
completely into anything that we do. As the first quotation indicates, it
is not as bad to be led astray through passion as it is to go through the
motions of a life without caring deeply about anything. Although
"passion is man's perdition," "it is his exhaltation as well." Still most
people are cautious, afraid of making a commitment to the wrong
thing. They're wary of passion; it's too risky.

Yet, a third point that Kierkegaard would make about passion is
that it is required for greatness. Certainly greatness in the aesthetic and
religious spheres requires passion, and probably in the ethical sphere as
well. The religious sphere, particularly, requires passion, since it
involves making a commitment to something irrational. Reason and
objectivity will never lead us to faith. Only passion, born of an inner
need of God in our lives, can motivate us to make the leap into the
Absurd which Kierkegaard calls faith. But we are all able to become
knights of faith, since we all are capable of passion:

> Faith is a miracle, and yet no man is excluded from it; for that
> in which all human life is unified is passion, and faith is a
> passion.[2]

This leads to the fourth, and perhaps most important, point which
Kierkegaard makes about passion. *It is the great equalizer of mankind.*
Not only is passion something which we are all equally capable of, but
it is the main requirement in order to have a life worth living. Unlike

---

[1] *Either/Or*, Vol. I, "Diapsalmata," in Bretall, *Op. Cit.*, p. 33
[2] *Fear and Trembling, Op. Cit.*, p. 77.

Nietzsche, who believed that only a few people are capable of greatness, Kierkegaard believed that the potential is in all of us.

Finally, not only is it impossible to have greatness without passion, but even individuality is threatened without it, according to Kierkegaard. When few individuals have passion, society is more susceptible to the development of the abstraction of "the public": "It is only in an age which is without passion...that such a phantom can develop itself."[1] Once the abstraction of "the public" is created, people will be content to defer to its voice rather than being concerned that their own voices are heard. In this way they will lose their own voices and become as much of an abstraction — a nothing — as the public itself: "More and more individuals, owing to their bloodless indolence, will aspire to be nothing at all — in order to become the public."[2]

This not only reminds us that, above all else, Kierkegaard is an individualist; but it also leads us to the last theme which will close our overview of Kierkegaard's philosophy: what Kierkegaard thinks is the "chief thing in life" which is "to win yourself, acquire your own self."

The "chief thing in life — win yourself, acquire your own self"

...if you have, or rather if you will to have the requisite energy, you can win what is the chief thing in life — win yourself, acquire your own self.[3]

What is the goal of life? According to Kierkegaard's philosophy of Individualism, we do not all necessarily want the same things out of life and that's fine. Our values may be very different. One person may pursue a life of pleasure, another world peace; and still another, like Kierkegaard himself, might try to discover what it means to be a Christian. But, no matter what path we choose, we should think of our lives as, above all else, taking the form of discovering and/or creating ourselves. This is the central goal of our lives as human beings, according to Kierkegaard: to "acquire" our own selves. Whether we are successful or not at achieving this goal determines whether we *really*

[1] *The Present Age*, in Bretall, *Op. Cit.*, p. 265.
[2] *Ibid.*, p. 267.
[3] *Either/Or*, in Bretall, *Op. Cit.*, p. 102.

exist as individual *selves* or whether we *merely exist*, that is go through the motions of a life *without becoming a self at all.*

As an existing individual, you are not born an already formed self; but you have the potential of becoming a self, and this should be your primary task in life. Others can't help you in this task. You are completely on your own, without any "eternal truths" to guide you, as you decide what is important to you as an individual. You only begin to fully exist when you commit to something.

A necessary condition for acquiring a self is to feel "a need for solitude." You can't determine what is important to you unless you spend time alone with yourself. It is an indication that you are in the process of acquiring a self that you need some time alone: "Generally the need of solitude is a sign that there is spirit in a man after all, and it is a measure for what spirit there is."[1] But many people can't bear to be alone, and it shows how far they are from becoming selves:

> The purely twaddling inhuman and non-human men are to such a degree without feeling for the need of solitude that, like a certain species of social birds (the so-called love birds), they promptly die if for an instant they have to be alone....these men need the tranquilizing hum of society before they are able to eat, drink, sleep, pray, fall in love, etc.[2]

Unfortunately, there are more people like these overly social beings who are afraid to be alone than there are people who appreciate the importance of solitude. As a society, we think of solitude as a form of punishment, rather than as a vital necessity for the development of the self:

> In the constant sociability of our age people shudder at solitude to such a degree that they know no other use to put to it but...as a punishment for criminals. But after all it is a fact that in our age it is a crime to have spirit, so it is natural that such people, the lovers of solitude, are included in the same class with criminals.[3]

---

[1] *The Sickness Unto Death*, in Bretall, *Op. Cit.*, p. 363.
[2] *Ibid.*
[3] *Ibid.*

To spend time alone and work on acquiring a self — to assume the tremendous responsibility for how your life develops — can be very stressful. You may, like Sylvia Plath, realize that you have many options and this may lead to anxiety about making a choice. You may stumble about, finding it difficult to sustain a single direction for more than a step or two. It's far easier to bend to social pressure and simply do what is expected of you. At some point, however, you may realize that societal pressures pull you in different directions. You will be guilty of "double-mindedness," unable to "will one thing" as you should. You will try to keep busy, hoping to ward off the quiet hour when you would have to face your despair over not knowing what you are living for, because you have avoided taking responsibility for your own life.

Your individuality, your self, is formed by your actions, by how you live. You can either take control of your own life and deliberately choose to live a certain sort of life, or you can let circumstances and others dictate your life for you. If you choose the second path, Kierkegaard says "[you] had no self, and a self [you] did not become." It would be incredibly sad to go through life without acquiring a self, without living up to your full potential; but, according to Kierkegaard, "unfortunately this is the sorry and ludicrous condition of the majority of men, that in their own house they prefer to live in the cellar."[1]

You may believe that you have acquired a self, but what you think of as your self may be merely a mask, or a series of masks, which you wear for others. If so, then you think of your self only in terms of *external* characteristics and believe that you can change this self as easily as one changes a coat. You may be very popular with others — you may even succeed "in astonishing the world" — yet:

> ...you will miss the highest thing, the only thing which truly has significance — perhaps you will gain the whole world and lose your own self.[2]

To acquire your self — which is "the chief thing in life" — you must choose *one* sphere of existence and passionately commit to it, even though there are no guarantees and even though others may not appreciate, or even understand, your choice. But in the end, you must answer to yourself alone; and the despair which you will eventually

[1] *Ibid.*, p. 346.
[2] *Either/Or*, in Bretall, *Op. Cit.*, p. 106.

feel, if you haven't decided and acted upon what is really important to you, will be far worse than the acceptance of the awesome responsibility of making such a decision.

Study Questions

1. Kierkegaard thinks it is important that one have a philosophy one could live by. How did he attempt to live according to his own philosophy?

2. Discuss the pros and cons of the idea of writing some books/ articles using pseudonyms to express truths about the world from particular limited perspectives and other works under one's own name to express one's own personal views.

3. Kierkegaard thinks it is extremely important to find "*the idea for which [you] can live and die.*" Do you think this is necessary to live a meaningful life?

4. According to Kierkegaard, what is needed to live is not *reason* and *objectivity* (which most people place great value upon), but *passion* and *subjectivity*. Do you agree? Disagree?

5. Discuss the debate between Individualism and Collectivism$_1$. Do you agree with Kierkegaard that each individual must choose his or her own path in life, that value is relative to the individual?

6. What does Kierkegaard mean by "truth is subjectivity"?

7. Kierkegaard seems to believe that objective uncertainty is a prerequisite for making a commitment to anything. Why? Do you agree?

8. Do you agree with Kierkegaard that the freedom we have to choose own our paths in life is both exciting and, at the same time, entails an awesome, frightening responsibility? Do most people try to avoid taking responsibility for their own lives? How?

9. Do you think that the way people choose to justify their lives basically comes down to the choice between leading an aesthetic, ethical or religious life? Can you think of any other options?

10. Kierkegaard thinks it is important to test yourself to see which sphere is right for you. Try to make up three tests which will help you to choose between: (1) the aesthetic and ethical spheres, (2) the ethical and religious spheres, and (3) the aesthetic and religious spheres.

11. Each of the three spheres has an heroic ideal. Kierkegaard gives names for two of them: the tragic hero and the knight of faith. Describe the characteristics of the aesthetic hero, the ethical hero and the religious hero. Which one do you most admire?

12. Does it trouble you that Kierkegaard depicts the religious sphere as irrational and distinct from the ethical sphere? What concerns does this raise? Does Kierkegaard have satisfactory responses to these concerns?

13. Do you agree with Kierkegaard that it is preferable to have "purity of heart" than to be pulled in different directions by conflicting impulses? Is it really possible to have "purity of heart"?

14. Kierkegaard seems to be saying that to have a successful life and the chance of achieving greatness, one needs both "purity of heart" and passion and that we are all capable of both. Do you agree?

15. What does Kierkegaard mean by "winning/acquiring oneself"? Is Kierkegaard right that this is the most important thing in life? To what extent does this view of Kierkegaard's reveal his bias towards individualism?

The Importance of, and Concerns about, Kierkegaard's Philosophy

It is appropriate to conclude this overview of Kierkegaard's philosophy with some thoughts about the originality and importance of Kierkegaard's ideas, and also why some people might find what he has to say to be very limited in value and/or disturbing. I shall argue that the two are related. The very aspects of Kierkegaard's philosophy which are most original and important have troubled a number of readers.

It has been mentioned that Kierkegaard can rightfully be considered to be the Father of Existentialism. Kierkegaard's beliefs that philosophy and life should be integrated, that we are free to choose not only between alternative actions, but even alternative value systems, that we are responsible for the choices we make and the selves formed in the process, that the realization of this will cause anxiety, that consequently most people will try to avoid taking responsibility for their own actions and lives, are all themes which became central to the movement known as Existentialism in the Twentieth Century. Kierkegaard is considered to be an extremely important and original thinker for having developed these thoughts ahead of others.

Yet there are concerns which people have with the views of Kierkegaard's which we associate with Existentialism. First, many people don't like the Individualism which is the foundation upon which this philosophy rests. Social scientists have convinced most academics, if not society at large, that we are essentially social creatures, that the philosophy of Individualism ignores this fact, and that it is even dangerous to encourage people to think that they should be entirely in control of their own destinies. They argue that to discover how to coexist peacefully, we must work together *collectively* to find guiding principles for our lives. One reason why the philosophy of Individualism has fallen into such disfavor, however, may be because it is mistakenly confused with Ethical Egoism, which, as we've seen, Kierkegaard certainly did not particularly recommend to anyone.

A corollary of the philosophy of Individualism is the idea that value is relative to the individual ("truth is subjectivity"). Most ethicists think that the view known as Ethical Relativism, particularly when held in the individual form, is not only dangerous but even undermines the very idea of ethics. What sense can we make of right and wrong, if it collapses into an individual just *thinking* something is right or wrong?

Let me define the term Ethical Relativism and the two forms it may take: the societal and the individual forms. Ethical Relativism is the view that there isn't a single standard of right and wrong, that when there is disagreement about whether an action is right or wrong, each side can be correct. The societal form of Ethical Relativism is the view that value is relative to the society in which one lives, that what is right for one society may be wrong for another. The individual form of Ethical Relativism is the view that value is relative to individuals, that what is right for one individual may be wrong for another. (Opposed to Ethical Relativism, in either of its forms, is Ethical Absolutism, the view that there is a single standard of right and wrong which all people should follow.) It would appear that the acceptance of the individual form of Ethical Relativism, unlike the societal form, does lead to the collapsing of something's being right or wrong into the individual just thinking it is right or wrong. Although the societal form of Ethical Relativism too has many problems,[1] it can maintain a distinction between an individual's thinking something is right and its being right, since what the individual thinks is right may be different from what the society as a whole thinks is right.

An important difference between Kierkegaard's philosophy and that of other existentialists with respect to the problem just raised with the individual form of Ethical Relativism is that Kierkegaard, unlike the others, is quite comfortable with Ethical Absolutism as an option for the individual. That is to say, the individual may choose the ethical sphere and in doing so commit to the idea that there is a single correct ethical code applicable to all. In this way Kierkegaard does give meaning to the ethical way of life, and it is a rather traditional meaning to which few would object. The only problem ethical absolutists would have with Kierkegaard is that he says that the individual does not *have* to live within the ethical sphere. But isn't it extremely difficult, perhaps even impossible, to refute Kierkegaard's position that there is no way to *prove* that the ethical sphere is the only correct perspective? As has been argued, the reasons people attempt to give to show that the ethical

---

[1] The societal form of ethical relativism faces difficulties like the following: If there is no clear majority opinion on an issue, say on capital punishment, does that mean that it is neither right nor wrong? And if the majority opinion changes over time, from the acceptance to the rejection of it for instance, does that mean that whereas capital punishment was once right, it is now wrong?

perspective is the only correct one already presuppose the correctness of the ethical perspective and so are circular.

Kierkegaard says that the most important choice a person has to make in life is whether "one chooses good *and* evil/or excludes them," in other words whether one chooses the ethical sphere, which will naturally be favored by society as a whole since it best protects its interests, or rejects it in favor of one of the other two spheres which allow the individual to assert his or her particularity over and above the universal. Generally it is the choice between the aesthetic way of life and the ethical with which the individual wrestles. Why should the individual feel compelled to act in the best interest of all when it is not in his or her own best interest? A classic novel which lays out this conflict is Andre Gide's *The Immoralist,* in which the central character, Michel, is alternatively attracted to both the aesthetic and ethical ways of life. One suspects that Michel is not labeled an immoralist so much for his often acting in a self-interested manner, as his inability to decisively choose one sphere over the other. He tries to avoid making the choice and taking full responsibility for his own life. That, according to Kierkegaard, is the real "sin" in life.

Besides the underlying Individualism and problems with the corollary to this view that value is relative to the individual, most people are also concerned that Kierkegaard's existentialist philosophy does not give us any guidance for how we should live our lives. Louis Mackay's summary of what Kierkegaard attempts to do for the reader in his writings points out the problem:

> Kierkegaard's poetic is a rhetoric designed to coerce its reader to freedom. By the impassioned detachment with which it marshals the resources of spirit, it lays on him the necessity to act and deprives him of any warrant for action except his own freedom. The Kierkegaardian corpus can neither be "believed" nor "followed": it is and was meant to be — poetically — the impetus, the occasion, and the demand for the reader's own advance to selfhood....[1]

We are used to philosophers not only giving us their view of the human predicament, but also advising us as to how we should live our

---

[1] "The Poetry of Inwardness," in *Kierkegaard: A Collection of Critical Essays,* Edited by Josiah Thompson, Doubleday & Company, Inc., Garden City, New York, 1972, p. 99.

lives. Kierkegaard does the first, but not the second. However, it is because the human predicament, as he sees it, is such that there is no single correct way for us to live our lives that he can not tell us how we should live. Still, that does not mean that he offers us no guidance in finding our own paths. He gives us the basic options, test situations which can help us to choose between them, and the advice that in order to "acquire our own selves," we must commit to one thing passionately.

Collectivists particularly will be unhappy that he does not tell us how we can best coexist with one another. He does not flesh out the ethical sphere, but leaves it up to other philosophers to do so. He does not see this as part of his self-appointed task, and there certainly has been no shortage of philosophers who have attempted to state what is ethically right. He also, as an individualist, is not concerned with politics, except to point out how harmful "the public" can be to the primary task each individual faces in life, to acquire his or her own self.

Kierkegaard spends time developing only one of the three spheres of existence which is a possible option for an individual: the religious sphere. He focuses on this sphere not just because it is his own personal choice, but because he does not think that any philosopher or theologian before him has properly understood what it means to be truly religious. Next to being the Father of Existentialism, Kierkegaard is best known for his unique view of the religious life.

Kierkegaard's view that religion is essentially irrational is radically different from others' views of religion before him. Others have thought of faith as believing in something for which we have insufficient evidence, which isn't necessarily irrational. Kierkegaard crosses the line from rationality to irrationality by defining faith as believing in something which is *logically impossible/absurd*: "The problem is not to understand Christianity, but to understand that it cannot be understood." (*Journal,* 1848) Furthermore, he doesn't apologize for the fact that the believer gives up his reason. He glorifies it. It is what makes faith so special and rare. Our ability to reason is not our most precious gift. Instead, it's our ability to feel *passion,* according to Kierkegaard.

This view of religion as essentially irrational is troubling to most philosophers, for whom reasoning is their basic tool. Kierkegaard responds that just because philosophers find it difficult, or impossible, to talk about faith doesn't mean that they should make light of it or try to turn it into something which it is not, just to make it easier to talk about:

> ...it is dishonest of philosophy to give something else instead of it and to make light of faith. Philosophy cannot and should not give faith, but it should understand itself and know what it has to offer and take nothing away, and least of all should fool people out of something as if it were nothing.[1]

I think that in Kierkegaard we finally have a philosopher who gets religion right by claiming that it is essentially irrational: "The realm of faith is...not a class for numskulls in the sphere of the intellectual." And, although this solves many problems for the believer, who no longer has to worry about contradictions, I also agree with Kierkegaard that saying religion is irrational makes believing in God more difficult, less comfortable, than most people would probably like. Kierkegaard sees as his mission to tell us what it *really* means to be religious, without mincing any words. Then it's up to us whether we want to believe in God or not. If more people reject religion, because they can't give up their reason, that's all right in his eyes. Far better for that to happen than to have the majority of people *think* they are religious, when they haven't a clue as to what it really means to be religious. Better to have only one truly religious person, in Kierkegaard's eyes, than to have millions of pretenders.

The greatest stumbling block to accepting Kierkegaard's view of religion, however, is probably not his depiction of it as irrational, as difficult as that may be for us to accept, but his claim that the believer may be required to do something unethical as a test of faith. This is certain to strike most people as an extremely dangerous thing to say, even if there is support for it in the Bible. Despite Kierkegaard's assurances that "it is only by faith one attains likeness to Abraham, not by murder,"[2] there is concern that some will feel that they have permission to kill others, as long as they claim that they were commanded to do so by God.

How concerned should we be, as a society, about this? There is certainly no test which one can give to another to determine whether a contemplated, or completed, unethical action is, or was, truly required

---

[1] *Fear and Trembling*, in Lowrie, *Op. Cit.*, p. 44.
[2] *Ibid.*, p. 42.

as an act of faith. The one who claims to be tested can't even know for sure. As Richard Popkin puts it:

> Each stands isolated on what he personally believes to be the Rock of Faith. And each has no way of telling whether it is madness or Divine Grace that provides the miracle of his faith.[1]

Is there no safeguard for society from violent persons suffering from a delusion that they are being tested by God, or, even worse, those who use the possibility of such a test as an excuse to get away with murder? Certainly there is a disincentive, and it applies equally as well to those whom Kierkegaard would consider to be genuine believers who commit unethical acts as a test of faith. All should be viewed as wrongdoers from the perspective of the ethical sphere and punished accordingly. Hopefully this will deter most people from performing unethical actions; and if not, we can at least protect ourselves from those who do by removing them from society.

We can draw an analogy between someone who practices civil disobedience and a knight of faith who commits an unethical act as a test of faith. Each one violates the universal laws which define the legal/moral realm and must pay the price for doing so, yet each believes he or she is right in violating the universal laws because there is something more important in that person's eyes than those laws. Each one takes a tremendous risk, and expects to pay the price for doing so if necessary, but hopes one day to be vindicated.

Of course there is an important difference between the one who practices civil disobedience and the knight of faith who is prepared to commit an unethical act as a test of faith. The first has not left the ethical sphere behind, but rather appeals to a *higher ethical principle* (typically that the current laws violate moral rights), whereas the second *leaves the ethical sphere* for another sphere altogether. Thus the second takes an even bigger risk, but that, according to Kierkegaard, is the nature of faith.

Before closing our discussion of Kierkegaard's unique depiction of religion, it should be noted that Kierkegaard's combining religion with his existentialist views is highly unusual and it leads to a third criticism many will have of the way he thinks of religion. Typically existentialists have been atheists and that is understandable when we

---

[1] "Kierkegaard and Scepticism," in Thompson, *Op. Cit.*, p. 372.

consider that a major theme of existentialism is that *we give life meaning; it is not given to us.* One would think that if there is a God, *He* gives life meaning, not we ourselves. What allows Kierkegaard to be the rare combination of a religious existentialist is that he claims that having a belief in God is a matter of our having a certain perspective on life, rather than discovering a truth which is "out there." For existentialists, *there are no truths "out there" to be discovered*; but there can be something that is true for us as individuals. So Kierkegaard has given up the objective content of religion — this is a consequence of his claim that "truth is subjectivity" — and, for many, this will be viewed as his "throwing the baby out with the bathwater."

In addition to his existentialist themes and his unique depiction of the religious sphere, there are at least two other original and important ideas which Kierkegaard introduced: (1) that there are three basic guiding principles a person can choose from — to live for oneself, for others, or for God — which are mutually exclusive and jointly exhaust the possibilities, and (2) that in at least one of his works, *The Sickness Unto Death*, "the whole murky realm of the subconscious is...opened up in so illuminating a fashion as to prove Kierkegaard one of the fathers of 'depth psychology'..."[1]

I would like to close with the observation that I know of no other philosopher who got as close to living in accordance with his own philosophy as Kierkegaard did. His life was a living demonstration that philosophy should not be a detached academic endeavor, that the whole point is "to find *the idea for which [you] can live and die.*" We can say, I believe, that Kierkegaard staked his entire life on his beliefs. He gave up personal happiness, true companionship with others, the understanding and approval of his contemporaries, to dedicate his solitary existence to revealing the human predicament as he saw it and to explaining his own choice of a guiding principle for a person's life. There was, and is, something heroic about such a life. As Kierkegaard said: "The man who can really stand alone in the world, only taking counsel from his conscience — that man is a hero."

---

[1] Bretall, *Op. Cit.*, p. 341.

Study Questions

1. Why do you think that some people are concerned about Kierkegaard's Individualism and the relativism which underlies his claim that "truth is subjectivity"? Should they be?

2. Do you agree with Kierkegaard that the most important decision a person makes in life is whether to choose "good *and* evil" or reject them? Does the pressure society imposes on the individual to conform to the ethical way of life lessen the chance that individuals who reject "good and evil" will actually do something unethical while attempting to lead an aesthetic or religious life?

3. Does Kierkegaard give us enough guidance for living our lives?

4. What concerns do people have about Kierkegaard's depiction of the religious sphere? From your understanding of religion, do you think the concerns stem from the nature of religion itself or is Kierkegaard wrong in his depiction of it?

Selected Bibliography

A Kierkegaard Anthology, edited by Robert Bretall, Princeton University Press, Princeton, New Jersey, 1946, 1973.

Fear and Trembling and The Sickness Unto Death, Søren Kierkegaard, translated by Walter Lowrie, Princeton University Press, Princeton, N. J., 1941, 1974.

Kierkegaard's Writings, Volumes I-XXV, Princeton University Press, Princeton, N. J., 1978- (some volumes still in preparation).

Encounters with Kierkegaard, A Life as Seen by His Contemporaries, edited by Bruce Kirmmse, Princeton University Press, Princeton, New Jersey, 1996.

Kierkegaard in Golden Age Denmark, Bruce Kirmmse, Indiana University Press, Bloomington, Indiana, 1990.

A Short Life of Kierkegaard, Walter Lowrie, Princeton University Press, Princeton, N. J., 1942, 1970.

Kierkegaard: A Collection of Critical Essays, edited by Josiah Thompson, Anchor Books, Doubleday & Company, Inc., Garden City, New York, 1972.